VAGUS NERVE

ACTIVATE YOUR VAGUS NERVE AND UNLEASH YOUR BODY'S NATURAL ABILITY TO HEALING YOURSELF. A SELF HELP GUIDE WITH EXERCISES FOR ANXIETY, DEPRESSION AND TRAUMAS FOR REWIRING YOUR BRAIN.

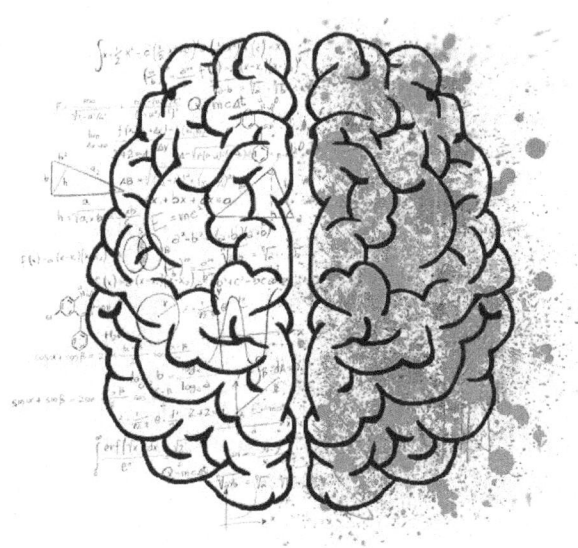

Published by K.D. Clive Collins

Table of Contents

Introduction

If you haven't heard about this nerve before, don't worry. While its existence has been known for some time, doctors and researchers didn't really understand it until recently. Modern research conducted on this nerve has led to many interesting discoveries.

So, what is the vagus nerve?

The name "vagus" is Latin for "wanderer". This means that the vagus nerve wanders and meanders throughout the body. It is a cranial nerve that runs throughout the entire body. It is associated to the parasympathetic nervous system (PNS). As such, it is the main highway by which the Central Nervous System (CNS) communicates with the PNS. As such, it is tremendously important in regulating all of the essential bodily functions that the PNS regulates.

Given the fact that it is so important, it is surprising just how overlooked this nerve actually is. So, sit tight because we are going to be discussing quite a bit of information here. You will surely find this to be insightful as well as fascinating.

We will begin by looking deep into two crucial components of the vagus nerve, the Pneumogastric Nerve and the Ventral Branch of the vagus nerve.

The Pneumogastric Nerve

Before modern research on the vagus nerve was conducted, the name it commonly received was the "pneumogastric nerve". It had earned this designation since the vagus nerve is responsible for the regulation of the heart, lungs and digestive tract.

As the pneumogastric nerve is responsible for ensuring the proper functioning of these systems through the PNS. The PNS relies on the pneumogastric nerve to relay the right information to and from the CNS and the brain. Yet, the fact that the pneumogastric nerve starts in the brain and works its way down into the lungs, heart and digestive tract, it essentially becomes one of the most important neural networks in the body. Needless to say, that if something goes haywire in the pneumogastric nerve, it can lead to serious consequences in the rest of the body.

The pneumogastric nerve begins in the brain and leaves through the medulla oblongata. Then, it basically runs straight through the middle of the body down the neck, chest and into the abdomen. The pneumogastric nerve has ramifications, or branches, that touch upon the main organ systems described earlier.

First, the pneumogastric nerve connects into the laryngeal nerve and then curves around the subclavian artery so that it emerges between the trachea and the esophagus. This is where it is able to regulate the functioning of the lungs. As such, this nerve enables the PNS to regulate breathing.

Next, the nerve runs down from the subclavian artery into the superior vena cava. From there, it moves on onto the bronchus before settling into the vagal trunk that passes through the diaphragm. It also connects into the carotid artery in which then allows it to link with the cardiac tissue. This is the point at which the pneumogastric nerve enables the PNS to hook up with the heart.

As the pneumogastric nerve makes its way down the esophagus and through the diaphragm, it is now able to link up with the digestive tract. This is what permits the PNS to regulate digestion.

As you can see, the pneumogastric nerve is truly an intricate piece of hardware which enables the PNS to regulate some of the most complex bodily functions. Needless to say, the body would not be able to function adequately without the pneumogastric nerve.

The pneumogastric nerve has the following branches which serve as means of communication among the entire routing of this nerve:

- Anterior vagal trunk

- Branches to the esophageal plexus

- Branches to the pulmonary plexus

- Hering-Breuer reflex in alveoli

- Inferior cervical cardiac branch

- Pharyngeal nerve

- Posterior vagal trunk

- Recurrent laryngeal nerve

- Superior cervical cardiac branches of vagus nerve

- Superior laryngeal nerve

- Thoracic cardiac branches

These branches are what enables the pneumogastric job to do its job effectively. When the system is firing on all cylinders, the communication flows effortlessly and regulation happens without a hitch. However, when there is a disruption in communication, or if the pneumogastric nerve becomes altered in any fashion, disruptions may occur leading to any number of potential medical conditions. Later on, we will dig deeper into these conditions.

The Ventral Branch of the Vagus Nerve

The emergence of Polyvagal Theory has allowed for a deeper understanding of the nervous system and its effects on the overall wellbeing of the body. Generally speaking, the vagus nerve is considered as one mega-unit which regulates a number of vital biological systems. We have covered this in-depth throughout the book.

At this point, we can dive straight into the discussion of Porges' Polyvagal approach explains the effect of the vagus nerve on the body. Since the vagus nerve is at the forefront of the PNS, it has a calming effect on the SNS.

Let's elaborate on that point further.

For instance, a person has been involved in a minor car accident, a fender-bender if you will. The incident itself is rather stressful though it does not bear any major consequences. As such, the individual is just shaken up and in need of some rest in order to get over what has occurred. In this example, the SNS kicked into high gear at the occurrence of the accident since the brain perceived a potential threat, that being the car accident. After closer inspection, there were no injuries, and everything proved to be rather innocuous.

If the PNS did not exist, there would be no way for the SNS to essentially shut off; the individual would remain at a constant state of stress and anxiety. Needless to say, they would not be able to sleep or eat due to the stress on them. This harkens back to the point we made earlier about prolonged stress and the effect it has on the overall nervous system.

After the brain has perceived that the threat is over, the PNS takes over and begins to bring back bodily functions down to normal parameters. This means that pulse and heart rate return to normal, blood pressure decreases, and the metabolism resumes normal operations. In the theory, all is well, and the individual makes a full recovery after a good night's sleep.

As a corollary, it is important to highlight the fact that sleep is a great equalizer. This is why you tend to feel sleepy after a significant spike in stress. Sleep allows the PNS to regulate body functions and bring the entire system back to normal. If you are unable to sleep, then the lasting effects will take much longer to become subdued thereby leading you to feel as if you had been hit by a train.

Based on the previous example, the ANS was seen as a mix of both active and passive roles. Of course, the active part only springs into action when there is the need for it, while the passive role hums along in the background.

That being said, the Polyvagal theory suggests that there is a third component of the system. A component which Porges called the "social engagement" system. In a way, this is a smart system that requires the removal of any perceived threat. What this implies is that we need to be able to discern when there is a threat and when there is not. When this discrimination occurs, it is not the "passive" side that takes over, but rather, it is the social engagement side of the equation.

So, how do these three systems work in tandem?

The SNS kicks into gear when there is a threat. Everything goes into high gear. The threat subsides and the brain determines the threat is over. Then, the social engagement system kicks in and alerts the SNS giving it the "all clear" signal. As such, the only thing that the SNS does is regulate the parameters of bodily functions; the SNS and the social engagement system work in an on/off basis. It should be noted that the default setting for the body is the activation of the social engagement system. The SNS is meant to be used only in case of emergency.

The ventral branch comes into play when the social engagement system is in control. The ventral branch essentially regulates everything that happens above the diaphragm in such a manner that the body is able to continuously regulate its responses.

In other words, the brain perceives a potential threat but then quickly discards it. The social engagement system clicks off and clicks back on almost instantly.

How does such a thing work?

For example, you are walking down the street at night and a person approaches. You are concerned that this may be a stranger who means harm. As you get closer, you realize it is a friendly neighbor. The warning issued by the brain did not last long enough for the social engagement system to be shut off and the SNS activated. However, the brain did issue a warning with alerted the social engagement system to be on standby. If the warning was real, then the SNS would kick in and the appropriate response would ensue.

According to this example based on the Polyvagal theory, the social engagement system is the default system for the human body. Consequently, this brings to light the fact that the SNS is only meant to be active for very brief periods of time. As a result, we can infer that prolonged periods of SNS activation can lead to a serious drain on the body's overall energy and wellbeing. Hence, it is vitally important to help the body calm down.

As we will discuss later on, this calming, or soothing effect can be achieved through the right stimulation of the vagal nerve. Moreover, it is helpful to look at this stimulation at a broader level insofar as the calming and soothing of the entire nervous system thereby leading the body to achieve proper balance among all of its functions.

That is why we would like to point out the importance of calming the nervous system throughout this book. That way you can begin to see immediate results. In fact, just by being able to take some time away from the main sources of stress in your life, you will be able to see a quick turnaround in the way you feel and the way your body reacts to the various stimuli around you. Of course, we will delve deep into this topic in due time.

In the meantime, it is highly recommended that you make an assessment of the various aspects that may be causing you to feel stressed out. Sure, there may be a stressor which you have little control over. For example, you may have very little control over your job. Still, you have control over the ways in which you can dissipate that negative energy that may be overloading your nervous system, in particular, the SNS thereby leading you to walk around with an overloaded PNS.

Chapter1: How Can Stress and Anxiety Affect Your Body And Life?

There can be situations when you just cannot act like before you used to because now anxiety its grip on you. It is the feeling of being afraid of the unknown. On a broader sense, anxiety comes in different forms like feeling worried, apprehension, nervousness, or feeling like everything is going out of control. Severe forms of anxiety can be extremely devastating and can have a great impact on your life and health.

Fear and panic are natural human emotions. Everyone has felt anxious for one reason or another. It is the feeling of worry, apprehension or panic in response to certain situations which is usually unsafe or uncomfortable.

Anxiety is a basic human emotion. Generally speaking, it is healthy and manageable to a certain degree. Because everyone experiences anxiety, it can be challenging to recognize and accept anxiety as a problem, however if you just ignore the symptoms of anxiety, you miss the chance to understand your life and yourself better. If you try to understand what your anxiety is telling you, you will have a better chance of overcoming the problem. In effect, you get to enjoy a better quality of life.

Is your anxiety helping you or has it become excessive and detrimental? We'll now try to learn more about anxiety and what you can do to help control the problem.

There are several 'listed' disorders that are all classified as 'anxiety.' Depending on the duration of the anxiety and its severity, it can actually lead to physical symptoms. When it manifests physically, it can cause the person to feel worn out, rundown, fatigued, it can cause pain in muscles and joints, it can lead to an increased risk of getting sick, and it can even increase the risk of heart attack, stroke, and a number of other health emergencies.

There are probably plenty of things that you have gone through in your life that caused you some level of worry. Maybe you had a test in high school that worried you. Even if you studied and felt confident that you knew the material, you might have worried about that test.

Maybe it kept you from getting a good night's sleep right before that test. Would that be considered anxiety?

It all depends. Since it interfered with your ability to sleep, some people could have been diagnosed as having mild anxiety. But most likely once the test was over you were able to get back to your normal routine and didn't worry about it anymore, and that wouldn't be classified as anxiety. More like stress.

We all experience stress throughout our life. It's quite natural and normal, but when you begin to worry excessively about certain things, especially things that you cannot control, then it becomes a problem.

As you deal with stress on a regular basis, whether it's because of financial pressures, schooling, relationship problems, worries about your job or finding work, or anything else, it can develop into anxiety over time.

What usually happens is that the worry starts to consume your thoughts. You begin thinking about the challenges you're facing on a regular basis. You could be thinking about the rent that's late while driving home from work knowing you can't possibly pay it right now.

You could be worried about the company you work for downsizing. You might be concerned about your adult child's well-being because he's out partying every night, doesn't seem to be taking any responsibility for his life, is getting himself into debt, and nothing you say or do – aside from paying those bills for him. -is making a difference.

When you try to fall asleep at night, when the TV is off and everything is quiet, and you can't shut the worry and stress off. You keep turning those fears over and over in your mind.

At some point in the middle of the night you might finally drift off to sleep but the alarm blares just two or three hours later. Now you're tired and have the deal with another day like that.

Multiply that night after night and the anxiety will continue to build even more because now you're trying to focus at work, impress the boss, or getting impatient with people around you.

You might snap at somebody then feel bad about it right away, and that's going to make things worse in your mind. Eventually you may feel tightness in your chest, shortness of breath at times, and have a difficult time getting anything done.

Over time you might withdraw from some of the activities you used to enjoy because you're spending all of your time worrying about everything, even though you're not actually able to do anything about them.

In time, you're living a completely different life with little to enjoy. That can lead to depression and a general state of worry about many other things, even those things that weren't a major concern for you in the past.

Chapter2: Inflammation, and What a Stimulated Vagus Nerve Can Do About it

Let's talk inflammation. Inflammation is something that happens within the body when there is a response to something that shouldn't be there.

Is all Inflammation Bad?

Not necessarily. In fact, inflammation is very important for making sure you respond to different stimuli within the body correctly.

With inflammation, you have either an injury, or a pain, or even an infection, and from this, you get more white blood cells, immune cells, and cytokines that are used for infection.

Inflammation is something that should be short-term, with redness, heat, swelling, and pain. But, in some cases, you might have inflammation happening within the body, without symptoms you normally don't notice.

When there is something in the body the brain recognizes as an invader, it starts the inflammation in the body. However, when not properly turned off, it can cause a lot of problems.

What conditions does it Cause?

Well, anything that yields an inflammatory response is a culprit here. For example, diabetes, heart disease, cancer, fatty liver disease, asthma, Chron's disease, IBS, and pretty much anything with inflammation as the cause is a part of this.

Food allergies and sensitivities are also seen here. Insulin resistance is another symptom of inflammation, hence why type 1 diabetes is often a result of inflammation in the body.

While some of the inflammation can be turned off quite easily, you'll realize that, with every single stimulus, it can actually make a lot of issues for people, and it can have a lot of problems that are very hard to fix if you're not careful.

People who are obese, or under a lot of stress, usually there is chronic inflammation there.

While you might notice it, most of the time you have to see a doctor to get some blood tests, including the C-reactive protein test, TMF alpha, and the IL-6, all of which are different chemicals that are within the body whenever you have an inflammatory response.

So, What Causes It?

Well, there are many different causes here, and the vagus nerve is actually a part of this. When the vagus nerve is properly stimulated, it sends out the neurotransmitters to tell the inflammatory response that it's over, the invader is gone, you don't need to activate, which causes a reduced response.

But, with a vagus nerve that's improperly stimulated, it can cause you to have overstimulation of the inflammatory response within the body, resulting in insulin resistance, heart disease, obesity, and also other conditions.

This is partially caused by your diet of course. Eating high amounts of sugars, carbs, high fructose corn syrup, and consuming a diet that's riddled with junk food is a part of the reason why you might have inflammatory responses, and the solution, in that case, is, of course, a diet change.

If you're stressed, and continuously activating the parasympathetic nervous system, your vagus nerve will be affected too. This, in turn, causes an inflammatory response in the body too, and hence, diseases will come forth too.

But, it's more than just the sugars. It's also how your vagus nerve is stimulated. When your vagus nerve isn't working, it won't control the inflammatory response, and oftentimes won't control the signals to the brain.

In many instances, when we're continually reducing our "flight or fight" responses, the biological markers will help with reducing inflammation.

When you see a doctor for inflammation, chances are they won't prescribe medications for that. That's because the way to combat inflammation can't always be handled with medication, and oftentimes, medications cause more side effects than help to the body.

The vagus nerve affects your heart rate, and also acetylcholine, which is a tranquilizer that you can administer to yourself simply through inhaling and exhaling, and from there, your parasympathetic nervous system will be activated.

When you activate this, you're essentially encouraging the "rest and digest" or the "tend and befriend" actions in the body. The "tend and befriend" actions within your body, of course, are those neurotransmitters that are activated.

When you activate your vagus nerve, you're basically turning off all of those responses you don't need in the body, and it'll help with inflammation.

Arthritis and inflammation

One aspect of inflammation that your vagus nerve can help to combat, is arthritis. Arthritis is inflammation of the joints, resulting in pain when moving the body. There have been tests recently which connected your vagus nerve to the inflammation in the body.

Rheumatoid arthritis, in particular, is oftentimes curbed with enough stimulation. When you implant a vagus nerve device into your body, it reduces inflammation and improves the outcome because it helps to inhibit cytokine production.

Rheumatoid arthritis is a chronic disease that involves inflammation, and it affects many people each year, in fact over a million people suffer from this condition, and research has been done to help with combatting the effects of this.

Most immunologists and neuroscientists have used new technology in order to look for the exact neural information that will tell us where inflammation is caused. There is an "inflammatory reflex" that's been discovered that our bodies have. This is actually a reflex that will cause cytokines to be produced.

Now cytokines are a part of increasing inflammation in the body, and are activated by an immune system response. Your vagus nerve essentially tells these cytokines to stop doing what they're doing, and it inhibits the overall production of these to help reduce inflammation in the body.

While more research needs to be done, it's been found that rheumatoid arthritis has been reduced by putting a tiny device in the body that triggers a chain reaction that helps to reduce cytokines, and thereby inflammation, creating a domino effect in the body when it comes to inflammation.

Most of the people can benefit from this right away are those with Parkinson's Alzheimer's, and Chrons, along with those with RA.

This device hopefully will help treat RA in the way that it should, and reduce inflammation not just in animals, but also in people. It can help with improving your immunity.

While there is still more research to be done, especially on improving this, this is a great way to improve the lives of others. We'll discuss in more detail what vagus nerve stimulations via this device in a later chapter, but for now, understand that arthritic conditions, especially rheumatoid arthritis, are oftentimes curbed, and there is a lot that this can do in order reduce this condition in the body.

Bioletic integrative medicine is now taking on studies involving vagus nerve stimulation these days to help people understand and stimulate their vagus nerve in order to help them, and it will cause not only fewer side effects, but it also is cheaper than other options as well.

Improving Autoimmune Conditions

Autoimmune disorders are disorders that occur when your body is acting on automatic to stimulate the immune system. However, usually autoimmune conditions stick around because, while the threat is long gone, your body doesn't realize it. The parasympathetic nervous system isn't properly stimulated, and this results in fatigue, inflammatory conditions, and you feel terrible most of the time.

These are oftentimes considered conditions you can't see, but you can feel. For example, while you can't see someone all the time with lupus, this is an autoimmune condition, and it makes people feel fatigued and tired.

The autoimmune responses are inflammatory responses and they are used by the body to protect itself, but the problem is, that protection oftentimes comes at a price.

But, your vagus nerve, when properly working, so work to help regulate this problem, making it easier for you to handle life. Autoimmune conditions don't need to lay waste to your body, but instead, by properly controlling all of this=, you'll feel better, and much happier too.

So How do We Combat This?

Inflammation is something you can't always see. It's why many times, people with inflammatory conditions are those who have "invisible illnesses" since they aren't visible to the naked eye, and sometimes not even to tests either, but they're there, and they're wreaking havoc on the body.

The best way to work on improving inflammation in the body is to stimulate the vagus nerve. When properly stimulated, it can reduce the inflammatory responses in the body, helping you feel better, and reducing the instances of this. This is oftentimes much harder than you'd think because many of us live stressful lives where we're always in the "flight or fight" modes in the body.

But if you take care of your body, and work to combat inflammation, it can help with the body, and reduce the instance of overstimulation of the vagus nerve.

When the vagus nerve is properly stimulated, your inflammation seems to almost magically go away. It works in-depth the neurotransmitters within the body, in order to help everything properly work.

Chapter3: Self Help Exercises
for Anxiety

Now that you know how the vagus nerve operates and why it is important for your health, let us now focus on its application. Many people are quick to use any means of vagus nerve activation that comes their way. As already mentioned, there are some techniques of vagus nerve activation that are helpful while others are harmful. You must be cautious not to use harmful techniques. Continuous activation of the vagus nerve using the wrong techniques may lead to chronic inflammation, which may be a source for more trouble. We have already looked at the negative effects associated with vagus nerve inflammation.

Breathing Techniques for Vagus Nerve Activation

To help activate the vagus nerve, you can adapt diaphragmatic breathing. In this type of breathing, the aim is to reduce the tension on the lungs and the heart. When you use this type of breathing, you allow yourself to take in air in slow bits that help reduce pressure. Diaphragmatic breathing helps in expanding the diaphragm. This is effective in reducing blood pressure and calming down nerves during anxious moments. The reduction of pressure and calming of nerves helps the body activate parasympathetic actions of the vagus nerve. The activation of parasympathetic action eventually leads to rest. Here is a step by step guide to diaphragmatic breathing.

Step 1: Position Yourself

When you want to breathe and calm down your nerves, you must align your body in a position that allows sufficient intake of air. In simple terms, your lungs should be open. If you try diaphragmatic breathing while you are lying on your belly or sitting in a bad position, you will strain; your body should be free enough to allow enough air into your lungs. The best positions include when you are standing upright or when you are seated upright. You can stand in an upright position and slightly spread your arms. This posture opens up your chest to allow sufficient air in. If you are seated on a chair or a mat, ensure that your back is in an upright position. This allows you to freely inhale the air.

Step 2: Inhale and Pause

After positioning yourself strategically, inhale a large chunk of air slowly and hold it in. You can hold your breath for about ten seconds or even more. Given that regular breathing includes 10 - 14 inhalations per minute, the diaphragmatic breathing usually involves around 6 inhalations per minute. When you inhale the fresh air, do not be in a hurry to let it out. Hold on to it for a few seconds; approximately 10, then release it gently.

Step 3: Slowly Exhale

After about ten seconds, you can now exhale and start the process all over. When you let out the air, you feel as if space has been freed up, and a weight has been lifted off your shoulders. The exhalation process helps clean your body of all negative energy. When you release the air, you allow your body to calm down and resume normal activities. It is important to note that this type of breathing should be well coordinated to work. If you do not allow yourself to calm down and try focusing on your breath, the effort may be worthless. As much as you want to enjoy your life and get rid of anxiety, you must try training your thoughts to focus on your breathing. You need to allow yourself to visualize the entire process.

Exercises That Activate Your Vagus Nerve

Exercising on a daily basis can also affect your vagus nerve. We know that physical activities are directly influential on your heart rate and blood pressure. These activities may moderate the heart rate or may increase it depending on your condition. While physical activities are effective in controlling the vagus nerve, not all activities will work out. In most cases, it is the gentle physical activities that do not require a lot of energy that works well in activating the vagus nerve. The two main physical activities used in vagus nerve activation include yoga and tai-chi.

Yoga: Yoga is a form of physical activity that involves stretching of the body muscles in combination with meditation and affirmation recitations. Yoga combines so many physiotherapeutic techniques in one session. If you want to benefit from the vagus nerve activation ability of yoga, you need to find the right yoga trainer. You can also perform yoga at home by using guided videos. One important factor to keep in mind when it comes to performing yoga is that the session should be mind calming. When performing yoga for vagus activation, try incorporating other techniques such as slow breathing, and meditation. To perform yoga well, you will need a quiet location with minimal disruptions. You will also need a yoga mat and a guide video. If you prefer performing among other individuals, you can get into a yoga studio around your home.

Tai-chi: Tai-chi is a form of wrestling technique originating from ancient China. The technique today is performed as a form of exercise. Tai-chi mainly involves slow horizontal movements with the hands placed in front of the practitioner. This type of exercise has been found to be calming and very helpful to individuals who wish to stimulate their vagus nerve. If you want to stimulate your vagus nerve, simply focus on working out on the slow movements. You can use a guided video to perform tai-chi, or you may choose to visit a studio near you.

Meditation for Vagus Nerve Activation

Meditation is one of the most important ways of activating the vagus nerve. Meditation can be used by any person, even those who have not attended meditation classes. As compared to tai-chi and yoga, which seem to be complex, meditation is a simple approach.

Meditation simply involves visualization. The practitioner has to visualize a certain environment that promotes calmness. The main aim of meditation in this process is to calm down the sympathetic action and activate the parasympathetic action of the vagus nerve. If you are capable of sending a signal to the brain that will initiate the actions of the parasympathetic nervous system, you will be in the right position to move on with your life.

To benefit from meditation, you need to choose the right type of meditation. There are many types of meditation. However, only a few are effective in calming down nerves and boosting your vagus nerve action. Some of the meditation techniques used to activate the vagus nerve include:

Mindfulness Meditation: In this type of meditation, the aim is to distract the mind from the thoughts that cause anxiety. When you practice mindfulness meditation, the focus is on yourself. You only think about yourself, your body, your environment, among others. If you want to enjoy the fruits of mindful meditation, you need to observe the rules for mindful meditation. First, during mindfulness, a person may discover some frustrating facts about themselves. In mindful meditation, you allow yourself to visualize yourself in a way that you have never done before. Therefore, all the benefits of the meditation should be protected by following the rules. One of the most important rules of this type of meditation is being non-judgmental. In other words, you are not allowed to judge yourself after observing your thoughts or feelings. You are required to embrace the truth about yourself. This action in itself promotes calming of nerves. Some people who suffer from depression only experience nervousness due to fear of being judged. However, if you can learn to accept your flaws through mindfulness meditation, you will not be shaken by anything. Mindfulness meditation teaches you to stand strong and believe in yourself no matter what the world may say about you. This is the attitude you need to overcome anxiety and depression. This attitude also promotes the parasympathetic activities of the vagus nerve.

Focused Meditation: Focused meditation is a type of meditation where the practitioner focuses their thoughts on a single object. In this type of meditation, you can choose any object in a room and simply focus on it. Focused meditation needs intense concentration. For instance, you can choose to focus on a chair or a wall. When performing focused meditation, you can't release your eyes from that piece of furniture. Use your mind to describe the chair and try looking at it based on different aspects. Think about its design, colors, shape, make, or any other aspect of the seat. Think about factors that make it special, how it holds weight, among others. This type of meditation is only intended to help you reduce the tension in your mind. After reducing the tension on your mind, the body can slowly reduce the sympathetic actions that are leading anxiety.

Peace, Love, and Kindness Meditation: This is the most ideal type of meditation for individuals looking to activate the vagus nerve. The fact that a person may be experiencing anxiety or depression means that they need an activity that will lead to the calming down of nerves. There is no better activity than peace, love, and kindness meditation.

In this type of meditation, you have to visualize yourself as a center of peace, love, and kindness to the world. In your mind, you have to visualize a world without violence or hatred. In this world, you are the main source of peace, love, and kindness. In this type of meditation, you visualize yourself extending kindness to people who need it. You stand out as an individual who embraces those who are weak. In your routines, you provide peace and kindness to people who are close to you and try to show them that the world can be a better place. You freely gift people who need help on the streets. You may also visit your enemies and extend a hand of forgiveness. Create a perfect world in your visualization and just indulge in that peaceful world for a few minutes. When you are done with your meditation, you will be in the right place to let go of all your fears and anxiety. This calming effect activates the vagus nerve, allowing you to live a normal life again.

Simple Step by Step Guide to Meditation

Step1: Prepare the Meditation Room and Tools

For meditation to be successful, you must find a quiet location without interruptions. You can meditate in your bedroom or in an open space. It is important that the meditation location has plenty of fresh air and that it allows you to enjoy peace during meditation. You will also need a meditation mat or a right-back chair. You may need some meditation music, but it is not compulsory.

Step 2: Position Yourself for Meditation

Before you start your meditation, ensure that you have enough time to complete the session. Switch off all interruptions such as your cell phone and only use your watch to set a reminder for timing purposes. Position yourself on the mat in a sitting posture with your legs right in front. Sit in an upright position and allow yourself to freely breathe in the fresh air. If you are using a chair, ensure your back is aligned parallel to the straight back of the chair. This allows your back to be in an upright position, which is perfect for free breathing.

Step 3: Close Your Eyes and Focus on Your Breath

To prepare your mind for meditation, you need to draw your concentration. The easiest way to start concentrating is by focusing on your breathing for about 5 minutes. Do not try controlling how you breathe. Just focus your thoughts on it and feel how the air goes in and comes out. This will raise your awareness of the environment and will allow you to concentrate on the moment.

Step 4: Get into Visualization

Once your mind has been prepared for the process, get deep into visualization. With any type of meditation, you can follow this process. You only start by preparing your room, position yourself, and prepare your mind. Once you are ready, you can now focus your mind on whatever it is that the meditation technique requires. For instance, in focused meditation, you may now open your eyes and choose to focus on the ceiling in the room. If you know that you will be performing focused meditation, ensure that there is something you can focus on in the room. Interestingly, you cannot lack something to look at and try to describe in your own understanding. If you are performing peace, love, and kindness meditation, you have to close your eyes and create the images in your head. You have to start visualizing your activities as the ambassador for peace to those who need it. It is much simple if you close your eyes and only focus on the meditation for a given period of time.

Natural Ways of Vagus Nerve Stimulation

Besides meditation, slow breathing, and yoga, there are other techniques of vagus nerve stimulation that are less harmful. Look at these techniques and use them to stimulate your vagus nerve when you are anxious or nervous.

Chewing Gum: Chewing gum leads to the secretion of CCK, a gut hormone that directly activates vagal impulses. This explains why people are likely to remain active for long hours while chewing gum. When a person chews gum, he/she can go for hours without taking food. This is due to the vagal impulses that CCK sends to the brain. The brain is tricked into thinking that the person is eating food. This trick can be used to reduce the sensory actions that lead to feelings of hunger in a person.

Eat High Fiber Foods: High fiber foods have also been found to be helpful in stimulating the action of the vagus nerve. Fiber foods are a good source of GLP-1, a satiating hormone that is responsible for the stimulating vagus impulses in the brain. This hormone helps slow down gut action and as a result, makes a person feel fuller for a long time. Some of the important high fiber foods include grains such as barley and peas. You can also rely on carrots, nuts, and potatoes, among others.

Tai Chi: We have already looked at tai-chi as one of the most effective ways of stimulating the vagus nerve. This is a 100% natural process since it does not involve the use of electronic gadgets. Tai-chi is known for its ability to increase heart rate variability; as a result, directly influencing the actions of the vagus nerve.

Gargling: Gargling may seem like child's play to many, but it is an important exercise that may influence your vagus nerve health. Gargling activates the vagus nerve and stimulates the gastrointestinal tract. Naturally, it is the vagus nerve that is supposed to activate the muscles behind the throat, allowing you to gargle. However, in a case where the action of the vagus nerve is slow, and the body needs some stimulation, self-induced gargling leads to the contraction of the muscles in the back of your throat, hence stimulating the vagus nerve. You can naturally stimulate your vagus nerve by gargling water before you swallow it.

Singing or Chanting: Another way of influencing the activity of your vagus nerve us through singing and chanting. Singing increases heart variability, just like it is the case with tai chi. Some of the best chants and songs include humming, mantra recitation, hymn singing, etc. These types of songs or any hyperactivity dance and song performance can influence your vagus nerve to a large extent. When you sing, you stimulate the vagus pump, which sends relaxing waves to the brain through the choir. If you chant or sing at the top of your voice, you activate the muscles behind the throat, which stimulate the vagus nerve for action.

Positive Socialization: Social relationships can make a person overcome some of the negative emotions that lead to anxiety. If you relate well with people, you are more likely to feel calm and relaxed even when the situations are tough. In one study conducted by the Michigan University Psychology Department, participants were asked to sit separately and think compassionately about their family and friends. The participants were also required to silently repeat passionate phrases such as ....may you feel happy, may you feel safe, may you live well, etc.

Compared to those controlling the research, the participants of the exercise showed an overall increase in positive emotions such as joy, amusement, serenity, interest, among others. These changes were associated with a sense of being connected. As a result, the participants experienced improved vagal activity as observed through their heart rate variability. If you want to be genuinely happy and live well in all situations, you must learn to embrace people. Bring people together and love your life with joy.

Laughter: They say laughter is the best medicine. When it comes to taking care of your mental and social health, there is no better option than laughter. Several studies indicate that laughter is the best medicine since it stimulates the vagus nerve. One research showed that yoga laughter led to increased heart rate variability among the participants. This goes to show that the heart can be affected by your laughter. When a person laughs, the back muscles of the thought are stimulated in the same way as gargling. This stimulation leads to the activation of the vagus nerve, bringing in a feel-good sense. You can improve your vagus nerve health by getting involved in activities that promote laughter.

Chapter4: Causes of Anxiety, Depression, And Inflammation

Relationship between inflammation, depression and anxiety

There is developing proof that inflammation can intensify or even offer ascent to burdensome side effects. The inflammatory response is a key part of our insusceptible framework. At the point when our bodies are attacked by microscopic organisms, infections, poisons, or parasites, the insusceptible framework initiates cells, proteins, and tissues, including the cerebrum, to assault these intruders. The principle technique is to stamp the harmed body parts, so we can give more consideration to them. Nearby inflammation makes the harmed parts red, swollen, and hot. At the point when the damage isn't confined, at that point, the framework ends up aggravated. These ace inflammatory variables offer ascent to "affliction practices." These incorporate physical, psychological and social changes. Normally, they wiped out individual encounters languor, weakness, slow response time, psychological impedances, and loss of craving. This star grouping of changes that happen when we are wiped out is versatile. It constrains us to get more rest to mend and stay disconnected so as not to spread diseases.

Be that as it may, a drawn-out inflammatory response can unleash ruin in our bodies and can put us in danger of depression and different sicknesses. There is a lot of proof cementing the connection between inflammation and depression. For instance, markers of inflammation are raised in individuals who experience the ill effects of depression contrasted with non-discouraged ones. Additionally, markers of inflammation can anticipate the seriousness of burdensome manifestations. An investigation that analyzed twins who offer 100 percent of similar qualities found that the twin who had a higher CRP fixation (a proportion of inflammation) was bound to create depression five years after the fact.

Specialists saw that their malignancy and Hepatitis C patients treated with IFN-alpha therapy (increments inflammatory response) likewise experienced depression. This treatment expanded the arrival of genius inflammatory cytokines, which offered ascend to lost hunger, rest aggravation, anhedonia (loss of joy), subjective impedance, and self-destructive ideation. The pervasiveness of depression in these patients was high. These outcomes add assurance to the inflammation story of depression.

Ensuing cautious investigations demonstrated that the expansion in the commonness of depression in patients treated with IFN-alpha was not just in light of the fact that they were wiped out. Utilizing a basic technique for infusing sound subjects with invulnerable framework intruders, specialists discovered higher paces of burdensome side effects during the ones which were presented contrasted with the fake treatment gathering. The subjects who were initiated to have an inflammatory response whined of indications, for example, negative state of mind, anhedonia, rest unsettling influences, social withdrawal, and intellectual weaknesses.

The connection between inflammation and depression is much increasingly strong for patients who don't react to flow antidepressants. Studies have demonstrated that treatment-safe patients will, in general, have raised inflammatory components circling at gauge than the responsive ones. This is clinically significant; a clinician can use a measure like CRP levels, which are a piece of a routine physical, to foresee the restorative response to antidepressants. In one examination, they found that expanded degrees of an inflammation particle preceding treatment anticipated poor response to antidepressants.

There are ecological components that reason inflammation and in this way, lift hazard for depression: stress, low financial status, or an agitated youth. Additionally, a raised inflammatory response prompts expanded affectability to stretch. The impact has been accounted for in numerous investigations in mice. For instance, mice that have gone under ceaseless flighty pressure have more elevated levels of inflammation markers. Strikingly, there are singular contrasts that make a few mice progressively impervious to push, in this way starting a more quiet safe response.

Depression is a heterogeneous disorder. Every patient's battle is extraordinary given their youth, hereditary qualities, and the affectability of their resistant framework, other existing real diseases, and their flow status in the public eye. Being on the disadvantageous finish of these measurements bothers our safe framework and causes incessant inflammation. The cerebrum is extremely responsive to these flowing inflammatory markers and starts "infection conduct." When the inflammation is drawn out by stressors or different vulnerabilities, the affliction conduct moves toward becoming depression.

Reasons for anxiety

Anxiety might be brought about by a state of mind, a physical condition, the effects of medications, or a blend of these. The specialist's underlying assignment is to check whether your anxiety is a manifestation of another ailment.

Current research on Anxiety Disorder

Much research is being done into what causes anxiety disorders. Specialists trust it includes a mix of components, including qualities, diet, and stress.

Investigations of twins recommend that hereditary qualities may assume a job. For instance, an investigation announced in plos ONE Trusted Source recommends the RBFOX1 quality might be engaged with the improvement of anxiety-related conditions, for example, summed up anxiety disorder. The creators accept that both hereditary and nongenetic variables have an influence.

Certain pieces of the cerebrum, for example, the amygdala and hippocampus, are additionally being considered. Your amygdala is a little structure somewhere inside your cerebrum that procedures risk. It cautions the remainder of your mind when there are indications of risk. It can trigger a dread and anxiety response. It appears to have an influence in anxiety disorders that include dread of explicit things, for example, felines, honey bees, or suffocating.

Your hippocampus may likewise influence your danger of building up an anxiety disorder. It's a locale of your cerebrum that is associated with putting away recollections of undermining occasions. It seems, by all accounts, to be littler in individuals who've encountered kid misuse or served in battle.

What causes anxiety disorders?

Anxiety is a psychological wellness condition that can cause sentiments of stress, dread, or pressure. For certain individuals, anxiety can likewise cause fits of anxiety and extraordinary physical side effects, similar to chest torment.

The definite reasons for anxiety disorders are obscure. As indicated by the National Institute of Mental Health, specialists accept that a mix of hereditary and ecological variables may assume a job. Cerebrum science is likewise being concentrated as a conceivable reason. The zones of your mind that control your dread response might be included.

Anxiety disorders frequently happen close by other psychological wellness conditions, for example, substance misuse and depression. Numerous individuals attempt to facilitate the side effects of anxiety by utilizing liquor or different medications. The help these substances give is brief. Liquor, nicotine, caffeine, and different medications can exacerbate an anxiety disorder.

Anxiety disorders are unimaginably normal. They influence an expected 40 million individuals in the United States, as indicated by the Anxiety and Depression Association of America.

What causes anxiety and anxiety disorders can be muddled. Almost certainly, a blend of components, including hereditary qualities and ecological reasons, assume a job. In any case, plainly a few occasions, feelings, or encounters may make side effects of anxiety start or may aggravate them. These components are called triggers.

Anxiety triggers can be distinctive for every individual, except numerous triggers, are normal among individuals with these conditions. A great many people discover they have numerous triggers. Be that as it may, for certain individuals, anxiety assaults can be activated for reasons unknown by any stretch of the imagination.

Therefore, it's imperative to find any anxiety triggers that you may have. Distinguishing your triggers is a significant advance in overseeing them. Continue perusing to find out about these anxiety triggers and what you can do to deal with your anxiety.

What are the anxiety triggers

Health Issues

A wellbeing analysis that is annoying or troublesome, for example, malignancy or a constant sickness, may trigger anxiety or exacerbate it. This kind of trigger is ground-breaking on account of the prompt and individual sentiments it produces.

You can help lessen anxiety brought about by medical problems by being proactive and drawn in with your primary care physician. Conversing with a specialist may likewise be valuable, as they can enable you to figure out how to deal with your feelings around your analysis.

Medications

Certain remedy and over-the-counter (OTC) medications may trigger indications of anxiety. That is on the grounds that dynamic fixings in these medications may make you feel uneasy or unwell. Those emotions can set off a progression of occasions in your brain and body that may prompt extra side effects of anxiety.

Prescriptions that may trigger anxiety include:

•Birth control pills

•Cough and blockage medications

•Weight misfortune medications

Converse with your PCP about how these medications make you feel and search for an elective that doesn't trigger your anxiety or decline your side effects.

Caffeine

Numerous individuals depend on their morning cup of joe to wake up; however, it may really trigger or exacerbate anxiety. As per one investigation in 2010Trusted Source, individuals with frenzy disorder and social anxiety disorder are particularly touchy to the anxiety-inciting effects of caffeine.

Work to curtail your caffeine admission by substituting noncaffeinated alternatives at whatever point conceivable.

Skipping Suppers

When you don't eat, your glucose may drop. That can prompt anxious hands and a thundering stomach. It can likewise trigger anxiety.

Eating adjusted suppers is significant for some reasons. It furnishes you with vitality and significant supplements. In the event that you can't set aside a few minutes for three suppers per day, solid tidbits are an extraordinary method to anticipate low glucose, sentiments of nervousness or fomentation, and anxiety. Keep in mind, nourishment can influence your disposition.

Negative Reasoning

Your mind controls quite a bit of your body, and that is positively valid with anxiety. When you're vexed or baffled, the words you state to yourself can trigger more prominent sentiments of anxiety.

On the off chance that you will, in general, utilize a lot of negative words when considering yourself, figuring out how to refocus your language and sentiments when you start down this way is useful. Working with an advisor can be fantastically useful with this procedure.

Budgetary Concerns

Stresses over setting aside cash or having an obligation can trigger anxiety. Sudden bills or cash fears are triggers, as well.

Figuring out how to deal with these sorts of triggers may need looking for expert support, for example, from a monetary guide. Feeling you have a buddy and a guide in the process may facilitate your worry.

Gatherings Or Get-Togethers

In the event that a room brimming with outsiders doesn't seem like fun, you're not the only one. Occasions that expect you to make casual chitchat or associate with individuals you don't know can trigger sentiments of anxiety, which might be analyzed as a social anxiety disorder.

To help facilitate your stresses or unease, you can continually bring along a friend when conceivable. But at the same time, it's critical to work with an expert to discover methods for dealing with stress that make these occasions increasingly sensible in the long haul.

Struggle

Relationship issues, contentions, differences — these contentions would all be able to trigger or compound anxiety. On the off chance that contention especially triggers you, you may need to learn compromise systems. Additionally, converse with an advisor or other emotional well-being master to figure out how to deal with the sentiments these contentions cause.

Stress

Day by day stressors like congested driving conditions or missing your train can cause anybody anxiety. Yet, long haul or constant pressure can prompt long haul anxiety and compounding manifestations, just as other medical issues.

Stress can likewise prompt practices like skipping dinners, drinking liquor, or not getting enough rest. These elements can trigger or intensify anxiety, as well.

Treating and avoiding pressure regularly requires getting the hang of methods for dealing with stress. A specialist or advocate can enable you to figure out how to perceive your wellsprings of stress and handle them when they become overpowering or hazardous.

Open Occasions Or Exhibitions

Open talking, talking before your chief, performing in a challenge, or even simply perusing so anyone might hear is a typical trigger of anxiety. In the event that your activity or diversions require this, your primary care physician or advisor can work with you to learn approaches to be increasingly agreeable in these settings.

Additionally, uplifting comments from companions and associates can enable you to feel increasingly good and sure.

Individual Triggers

These triggers might be hard to distinguish, yet a psychological well-being authority is prepared to enable you to recognize them. These may start with a smell, a spot, or even a tune. Individual triggers remind you, either intentionally or unknowingly, of an awful memory or awful accident in your life.

People with post-awful pressure disorder (PTSD) as often as possible experience anxiety triggers from ecological triggers.

Distinguishing individual triggers may require some serious energy, yet it's significant so you can figure out how to conquer them.

Chapter5: Vagus Nerve Dysfunctional Signal

The vagus nerve may dysfunction when it is exposed to extremely stressful conditions. Sometimes, you may not be able to tell when the nerve is dysfunctional. Normally, the symptoms associated with vagus nerve dysfunction are also associated with other conditions. You may be fooled to think that you are suffering from a different infection, yet it is due to nerve damage. We have observed that the vagus nerve supports several activities and that all the activities are vital in your daily routine. A slight dysfunction of the nerve can put most of these activities to a halt or may affect the way you function.

There are two main causes of vagus nerve dysfunction: vagus nerve damage and vagus nerve inflammation. At this level, all you have to note is that damage may lead to many health complications. The symptoms for vagus nerve damage may be very similar to the nerve stressing ones.

Vagus nerve stress can happen at any time or any day. As we delve deeper, we will be looking at environmental and social factors that can stress your vagus nerve. Knowing that the nerve can be stressed should raise the alarm on how you cater to your vagus nerve. It is necessary that you protect your nerve from any damage. All instances that may lead to the stressing of your vagus nerve must also be avoided.

Before we look at the symptoms of vagus nerve dysfunction, we should try and find out the possible ways of proving the dysfunction. As already mentioned, the symptoms for a dysfunctional vagus nerve are the same as those for a damaged nerve. The only way to be sure whether your nerve is dysfunctional or damaged is to undergo medical tests. There are several tests that can be used at a local health facility or even at home.

Doctors use the gag reflex test to determine the response of the nerve. In this test, a doctor will insert some soft tissue, maybe a cotton bud into your throat, and try to swab it on both sides. Normally, if the vagus nerve is functioning properly, the patient is supposed to feel a tickling sensation resulting in a gag. However, if the nerve has been damaged, the person may not feel anything. Other advanced tests can be used to determine the state of the vagus nerve, as we will see later on. There are different tests for diagnosing a damaged nerve, and there are individual tests that you can perform at home. However, this particular test is ideal for any individual who wishes to gain some certainty about the functioning of their vagus nerve. Before you jump into treating the nerve dysfunction, try to check the cause and make sure you have certainty that it is damaged.

Early Symptoms of Vagus Nerve Dysfunctional

There are clearly observable symptoms of vagus nerve dysfunction. However, some of these symptoms may be very diverse such that, most people never associate them with the vagus nerve. In most cases, the symptoms are associated with common conditions. If you realize that you are experiencing several of the following symptoms, it is wise to get a doctor's opinion on the health status of your vagus nerve.

•   Difficulty Speaking or Loss of Voice: We have mentioned that laryngeal is the extension of the vagus nerve that extends directly to the voice box. This nerve is important in coordinating and controlling the activities of the voice box. If the nerve is damaged, muscle contraction and expansion becomes a complex duty. For this reason, any person suffering from vagus nerve damage or dysfunction is likely to suffer from voice problems.

•   A Voice That Is Hoarse or Wheezy: This is still a part of the integral functions of the laryngeal. If you find out that your voice is getting horse or wheezy, the chances are that your vagus nerve has become dysfunctional. With that said, it is important to note that most people experience a wheezy voice during many instances. A simple cold could lead to a wheezy voice. This is the reason why it is important to get an opinion from the doctor before jumping into a conclusion about any symptom.

• Trouble Drinking Liquids: We have observed that the vagus nerve plays an important role by providing motor action to some parts of the body. The most integral parts of the body where the nerve plays such a role include the pharynx. The laryngeal extension of the vagus takes action on the pharynx and stylopharyngeus muscles that affect the swallowing of food. We have determined that the vagus nerve has an effect on the muscles that determine taste and also affects the production of certain enzymes. If you start realizing that you cannot swallow drinks, the chances are that your nerve is dysfunctional.

• Loss of the Gag Reflex: When you touch an object at the back roof of your mouth, the back muscles of the throat close automatically. This is what we refer to as the gag reflex. The gag reflex is very important since it helps a person swallow food and drinks. The reflex also plays an important role in separating the food pipe and the air pipe. In other words, if you did not have a gag reflex, the chances are that foods might find their way into the lungs. The fact that the vagus nerve controls your gag reflex means that any dysfunction of the nerve may lead to a lack of gag reflex. This option also provides one of the most reliable ways of testing your vagus nerve health. If you try touching the roof of your mouth close to the throat, you must experience an automatic closure of the throat muscles. This will give you a guarantee that your vagus nerve is still functional.

• Pain in the Ear: A branch of the vagus nerve known as auricular nerve extends to the ears. This nerve plays an important role in controlling the hearing of an individual. As a matter of fact, the auricular directly influences your sound senses. You may never be able to perceive sound well if the nerve is damaged. Pain in the ear is one of the obvious signs that the vagus nerve has been damaged. This is because the pain can only be caused by a fracture on the nerve.

• Unusual Heart Rate: The fact that the vagus nerve is linked to the heart means that any damage to the nerve may directly affect the heart rate. The cardiac extension of the vagus nerve determines the contraction of the heart muscles. This extension also helps in maintaining a steady flow of information between the heart and the brain. If the sensory nerves of the heart fail to function, the chances are that the heart may fail or may show abnormal rates. The normal heart rate is around 72 bits per second. In the case where the rate goes beyond 72, the patient should either be involved in cardiovascular exercises or the vagus nerve may be exposed to stress leading to the increased production of adrenalin.

• Abnormal Blood Pressure: We have established that the vagus nerve also affects the constriction of blood vessels. If the nerve is stimulated or under stress, it may lead to the constriction of blood vessels. Given that pressure may also lead to an increased heart rate, this simply means that overstimulation of the nerve may cause increased blood pressure. When the heart is pumping at fast rates, yet the blood vessels have been constricted, the blood pressure is bound to increase. Such occurrences may lead to heart attacks or loss of consciousness. If you experience increased blood pressure constantly, you need to try and figure out the triggers. If your pressure is caused by vagus nerve stimulation or failure, the chances are that your nerve is malfunctioning. However, you should also remember that no all blood pressure issues are associated with the vagus nerve. Some of the blood pressure issues are associated with other lifestyle diseases.

•   Decreased Production of Stomach Acid: We have also established that the vagus nerve works in conjunction with endocrine glands to ensure that food is digested. Before endocrine glands can produce the necessary enzymes that are needed in food digestion, they must receive signals from the autonomic nervous system. The most central part of the anatomic nervous system is the vagus nerve. If you realize that you are experiencing some of the symptoms of low stomach acids such as bloating, belching, heartburns, among others, you should start observing for other signs of vagus dysfunction. These symptoms may appear in short intervals if your vagus nerve is ailing. If the nerve is completely damaged, you may experience such conditions continuously.

• Nausea or Vomiting: Nausea and vomiting are also some of the symptoms that indicate high levels of stomach acid. If the vagus nerve is affected, it is possible to suffer from nausea and such symptoms. This is because the regulatory tissues that control the production of stomach acid are not functioning properly.

• Abdominal Bloating or Pain: The abdomen is the final destination of the vagus nerve, with the final ending touching the spinal cord. The fact that the nerve is extended to the lower abdomen means that if it is affected, you may experience some defects in your body. Given that the nerve plays an important role in controlling stomach muscles, it can be painful, leading to abdominal pain in some people.

Advanced Symptoms of Dysfunctional

The above symptoms are general and can apply to any person who has a dysfunctional vagus nerve. However, there are cases where the nerve is severely wounded or is completely damaged. In such cases, the symptoms tend to advance. In most cases., when the damage is, to a large extent, the focus is on diseases that may result from the vagus nerve damage.

In the above, we only focused on general symptoms that may relate to any problem to the nerve. However, as you advance to the next stages, you realize that the extent of damage to the nerve may cause some serious illnesses. There are two main diseases that doctors have linked to vagus nerve damage. We will look at these diseases in detail as we advance. In this , we only want to look at the symptoms and how they may be a way of showing that you have a dysfunctional vagus nerve. If you cannot detect or diagnose a defective vagus nerve, you may end up living in pain for a long time without being able to tell the cause. You may even be misdiagnosed by doctors if you do not know the right information about that condition. The two main conditions that may affect a person due to a damaged vagus nerve include gastroparesis and vasovagal syncope.

Gastroparesis

Several research findings have shown that there is a direct link between gastroparesis and vagus nerve damage. This is a condition that severely affects the involuntary contraction of the digestive system. As we had mentioned, the vagus nerve, in conjunction with ANS facilitates the parasympathetic functions of the body. Some of the parasympathetic functions include involuntary contraction of the digestive system. In simple terms, when you suffer from a damaged vagus nerve, you may never enjoy parasympathetic actions of defecation. The stomach does not empty properly, and this leads to a continuous pile up of dirt. Some of the common symptoms of this condition include

• Nausea or Vomiting: In the symptoms above, we mentioned nausea and vomiting. However, this case is much worse and severe. In the case of gastroparesis, the patient is unable to let out most of the food eaten. This leads to nausea and vomiting of foods long hours after eating. In normal vomiting situations, a person just vomits a few minutes after eating. However, in these advanced cases of gastroparesis, the victim is likely to vomit after very many hours of waiting.

•   Loss of Appetite: Most people who suffer from gastroparesis, often eat a little food and constantly lack appetite. This condition makes a person feel full even when they are hungry. Patients suffering from this condition may either completely lack appetite or feel full after eating just a little amount. However, there are many other conditions that may still lead to a lack of appetite. Do not be quick to jump to conclusions just because a person lacks appetite. If you feel that you are suffering from a lack of appetite, investigate all the possible causes. You may also have a doctor test you for vagus nerve dysfunction.

•   Acid Reflux: Acid refluxes will just occur as it is the case above. However, in this case, they will be much more severe and may be recurrent.

•   Abdominal Pain or Bloating: The other direct symptom of gastroparesis is bloating and abdominal pain. The vagus nerve spreads to the lower abdomen, having an influence on your excretory and sexual organs. This means that any damage to the nerve may directly affect your sexual health or your digestive health. Such conditions will often lead to abdominal pain.

• Unexplained Weight Loss: There are several reasons why a person suffering from gastroparesis may lose weight. First, such individuals do not eat as much as they should eat. This means that the body is denied some of the essential vitamins. Further, the body does not fully digest the food consumed. In most cases, the food has to come out through vomit. Such issues often lead to a loss of weight in most patients — this a distinctive observation for the severe stage of vagus nerve damage. In the early symptoms, the patient may experience digestive complications, but they are not to the extent of affecting personal weight. In essence, those who suffer from the early stages of vagus nerve damage still have a choice to make on the types of foods they want to eat. They may still eat without vomiting. However, the stage where gastroparesis develops, it is almost impossible to manage the effects associated with eating.

• Fluctuations in Blood Sugar: If you do not eat properly, you will end up affecting your blood sugar. The human body's blood sugar is balanced by the food being processed into glucose and absorbed into the system. However, if the stomach is not in a position to digest all the food that you eat, you are likely to encounter severe shortages in energy and blood sugar.

We have mentioned that some traditional treatment methods advocate for the removal of the vagus nerve through a process known as vagotomy. In this process, part of the nerve was cut off to help patients who suffer from increased stomach ulcers.

However, it was realized that this process had several side effects. One of the most severe side effects associated with the vagotomy was the development of gastroparesis. It was realized that patients who underwent the process suffered advanced symptoms only associated with this condition.

Vasovagal Syncope

It is common for the vagus nerve to overreact to stress or stimulation. In the case of an overreaction, the vagus nerve may develop a condition known as vasovagal syncope. This condition can lead to a sudden drop in heart rate and blood pressure. If a person undergoes an extreme stressing situation that directly affects the vagus nerve, the drop in pressure may result in loss of consciousness (fainting). This is the condition that is known as vasovagal syncope. It is important to remember that the vagus nerve plays a central role in stimulating several muscles in the heart that directly affect your heart rate. If the nerve is overstressed, it may lead to a slowdown in the body processes leading to this condition.

Some of the extreme pressure events that can lead to vasovagal include:

·   Exposure to Extreme Heat: Exposure to extreme heat all over sudden or for long hours may lead to excessive dilation of blood vessels. The dilation, in conjunction with the reduced pressure due to stress, may result in low blood pressure and a slow heart rate. This scenario is likely to lead to a loss of consciousness.

·   Fear of Bodily Harm: Most people react differently to emotional situations. The emotion of fear has the strongest effect on the vagus nerve. When a person is afraid, excessive levels of adrenaline are produced to start the fight or flight state of the body. In this state, the vagus nerve is under extreme pressure. If someone was to startle you in the dark, you might undergo this type of excessive pressure. This may lead to a sudden drop in blood pressure and lead to a sudden loss of consciousness. In some people, the same action may lead to increased heart rate, increased blood pressure, and body heat. It is common to see people sweating under intense fear.

·   The Sight of Blood or Having Blood Drawn: If you have fear for blood or if you fear needles, you may also undergo vasovagal syncope. This is common when a person sees blood for the first time. Since the picture blood creates a situation of intense fear, you are likely to stress the vagus nerve. This may lead to a sudden drop in blood pressure and heart rate, and as a result, lead to fainting.

•   Straining: One of the ways to detect that a person is suffering from vasovagal is by observing the strain they go through. If you find yourself straining to have bowel movements, the chances are that you are suffering from vasovagal syncope. The pressure on the vagus nerve usually affects the digestive system and may lead to reduced intestinal action.

Chapter6: Trauma

What is trauma? The term is rather loosely defined and is generally talked about in terms of both emotional and psychological trauma. Psychological trauma focuses on the health of the mind, while emotional trauma revolves more around feelings.

Trauma is more than just stress. Our bodies return to normal functioning after a day or two when we experience a stressful moment or event. In cases where the person has been traumatized, their body does not return to that normal state. Scientists have even found through brain scans that our brains are changed when we are experiencing something traumatizing. There is a biological component to trauma, changing us physically on the inside. This has been clearly shown through MRIs of brains before and after a traumatic event.

It is important to distinguish between average, manageable stress versus real trauma. We can tell the difference by how quickly we return to normal after the event.

Is the traumatic event still affecting your everyday life? Are you upset faster or more often? Are your reactions appropriate to the actual situation affecting you right then? Are you upset an extraordinary length of time? Do you have difficulty coming back to a calm state? Do you have flashbacks of the event that are startlingly realistic? Do you feel burdened or chained by these thoughts?

Even if we do not realize it, we can be experiencing trauma. It has sometimes been described as frozen in an active state of emotional intensity. No matter what causes it, emotional trauma happens when you experience something you were not expecting, were not prepared for, and had no way of preventing it. You were trapped in that event, and it overwhelmed you.

Psychological trauma involves more of an actual physical event, going through a natural disaster perhaps, or an assault or accident. Even a sports injury, when unexpected and devastating, can cause psychological trauma.

Any number of things can cause either psychological or emotional trauma. There are certain symptoms you can look out for if you think you have been traumatized. A few of them are:

Eating or sleep disturbances

Chronic unexplained pain

Depression or anxiety

Emotional numbness

Withdrawal from family relationships

Inability to concentrate

Feeling distracted

This is by no means an exhaustive list. If you believe you might be experiencing the symptoms of trauma, please get help. Perhaps the next few chapters of this book will help you start your journey back to a place of health.

Polyvagal Theory and Trauma

The polyvagal theory has had a profound impact on how we treat emotional trauma, as well as many psychosomatic disorders where physical symptoms arise from emotional or mental factors. In the past, much of the theory of therapy dealt with specific events, figuring out what had happened in the patient's past and how to deal with those issues. While I am not here to argue with that model of therapy, and this book is not about therapeutic practices in the professional field, the polyvagal theory approaches patient therapy in a slightly different way.

Using the polyvagal theory, you could think of your nervous system as employing three very different warriors in your body's defense.

The first is the Viking warrior, the fighter. He slashes and burns without thinking, going for the most effective route through any barrier that presents itself. This warrior is bold and brash and is thinking only about defense.

The second is Flash, the comic book superhero. His greatest superpower is running lightning fast and for a long time until the danger is far behind. He is thinking of only one thing - the swiftest, straightest path to getting away. Far away.

The third is a ninja. Stealth is key to this warrior. His defense is most often to lie in the shadows, to wait unseen, to immobilize until the danger has passed by. He is entirely consumed with remaining in the shadows.

Each of these warriors usually fights alone. Although the first two will sometimes blend a bit, working in conjunction with one another as if they were on the same wavelength, the ninja only works alone.

These warriors are meant to be temporary rules of our body, but trauma takes these three warriors and sets them in charge of the body full time. Instead of being hired for a temporary job, they unpack, settle in, and make themselves at home and in charge for the long haul. They become the masters instead of the servants.

Next, we will be talking about how these warriors accomplish the takeover – what gives them the power to remain in charge? And how can we take that power back?

When Neuroception Goes Wrong

What counts to humans as a state of danger? What do we see as dangerous? This seems like a straightforward question with a very simple answer, but in reality, it is not. There are some things that are instantly and universally recognizable as a danger. For instance, we would see a lion prowling around our backyard as a dangerous situation and depending on our confidence level, we would either fight the lion or flee from it. We would see an approaching tornado as a dangerous situation, and we would instinctively flee.

There is another world of sensory input though, one called neuroception. Neuroception is the automatic detection of a threat as sensed by the automatic nervous systems in our bodies. We interpret tiny things around us and incorporate them into our overall sense of safety, whether we realize we are doing it or not. If a person is lower on the vagal ladder, they may interpret neutral faces as angry, for example. This is because our nervous system is always vigilant for threats, and if it is already in a hypervigilant state, then it is going to interpret things around us to be dangerous more often than not.

When someone has faults in their neuroception, they will feel isolated. Partly because they do not know who to safely approach as a friend due to misreading other people, and partly because they are not approached as often by other people due to sending out signals that conflict or do not look quite socially acceptable. The phrase sending out the wrong signals is really quite literal here.

Telling someone just to "act friendly," while technically accurate, is not quite enough for everyone. The person cannot show others that they are a friendly person if they do not understand the facial gestures and societal signals that indicate openness and a willingness to being approached as a safe person. For someone with a damaged or misaligned neuroception system, this must be taught.

This can be done through one-on-one therapy, personal research and study, or mingling regularly with a loved and trusted group of people who understand that this person needs help.

A man named Ravi Dykema put together a wonderful list of helpful things to keep in mind that fit nicely in the polyvagal theory regarding neuroception.

Do:

Make eye contact when you feel safe.

Do express with your face.

Do modulate your voice (use expression).

Do adjust your circumstances to feel safer – for example, move to a quieter place.

Do adjust your focus to things that will make you feel safe, such as focusing on something familiar or comforting.

Do play a musical instrument.

Do try moving into social relationships instead of away, as a way to reduce slight anxiety.

Don't:

Don't try to extend yourself physically while having a deep conversation. You're very likely to read all the cues from the other person in the wrong way.

Don't allow yourself to become isolated. Don't seek isolation in order to feel safer. Stay connected with other people.

Don't force yourself to interact when you aren't feeling safe enough. Bring yourself to a state of safety and then seek that interaction with other people.

Don't discount what your gut is telling you. Pay attention, learn from what your body is telling you.

Don't resort to fight or flight when it involves loved ones. Get to a safe place, but don't damage the relationship with your loved ones in order to do so.

Don't allow yourself to take on a flat affect when you want the people around you to feel safe with you.

Do not let social media or internet platforms to become a substitute for interaction with people face-to-face, or even on the phone.

Don't assume that the worst example of someone else's behavior is their "true" self. The moments when they show peace, calm, and caretaking behavior are also just as "true" for them.

This list can be used to relearn social behaviors, to reconnect with others around you.

As the main component of the parasympathetic system, the vagus nerve is an integral part of the body's autonomic response to fear, and thus its health is paramount in being able to self soothe after a traumatic or startling event. Once the danger has passed, the vagus nerve needs to be able to tell the body this, so that it can calm itself and enter back into a state of rest.

By stimulating the vagus nerve (or waking it back up once our sympathetic nervous system has shut it down) we then flood the body with calming enzymes, sending the signal to the body that the danger is gone, and relaxation can happen again. This has been proven to alleviate stress and calm anxiety. Emotional trauma can damage, or retrain, the receptors that tell our bodies danger has passed. These traumas can trick the receptors into feeling as if the danger is still there, or that something benign is a signal of something dangerous.

When discussing the attempt to heal, or retrain, the vagus nerve, it is important to remember that the feeling of safety is more important than actual safety when it comes to signals being sent to the vagus nerve.

For example, a young boy is walking down the street outside his house minding his own business. Suddenly two large dogs appear from an alley nearby and begin to chase him. They catch him and cause him severe injury. He is only saved by the heroic actions of a passerby who steps in and fights the dogs off. Follow that same boy several months later, and he is recovered from his physical injuries. Again, he is walking down the street outside his house minding his own business when suddenly a dog approaches from an alley. This dog has its ears up, its tail in a neutral position, and sits when he sees the boy approach. The boy does not think, he just reacts, running as fast as he can in the opposite direction. The earlier traumatic event with the other pair of dogs can easily send the boy running from this second situation as well. His body has learned to interpret any dog he sees as the same life-threatening event as he experienced that first time. It is an involuntary, sympathetic reaction governed by his sympathetic nervous system. In other words, he literally cannot help himself.

The only course left is to retrain the nerves to interpret his world based on the ventral state of the vagus nerve rather than the dorsal state.

These instances so far have been based on things that happen to us, events that perhaps were no one else's fault, and certainly not of our own making.

Next, we are going to talk about something that is also not the fault of the victim, but holds a dearer, more traumatic price because it comes at the hands of someone who ought to be more caring, who ought to be loving.

Emotional Abuse and Trauma

Sometimes faulty neuroception or an emotional trauma that changes our perceptions comes from an event that happened to us, but other times, unfortunately, emotional trauma comes directly from someone who claims to love us. When someone who ought to be taking care of us engages in emotionally abusive behavior, we can internalize it, becoming so used to their behavior that we mistakenly think it is normal and begin to judge all other behavior by that abusive measurement.

This is not your fault. This is the body's natural method of finding a way to survive. However, you can break out of the cycle of emotionally abusive behavior by first recognizing the truth, and then second, getting help to get out. These sound so easy to accomplish, and yet in reality they are not. The person who can overcome what their own body is telling them is showing courage and resilience. But first you must come to a place where you recognize that your body is just doing what it can to survive, and once that recognition takes place, you can then take charge and reteach your body what a healthy emotional state actually looks like.

Signs of emotional abuse can be subtle, and the abuser often is a master at manipulation, using your own needs against you to create a sense of dependence on themselves.

You can spot them though, so here are some of them.

Humiliating behavior, negativity, and criticism in the extreme. This is not just making a mistake or wording something awkwardly, but saying things designed to humiliate or to paint you in a negative light. Nicknames that actually are cruel or demeaning – "cutie-patootie" is a cute nickname, "fatty" is not. Publicly embarrassing you, joking about things that make you look foolish or are at your expense, sarcastic remarks and then telling you that you are being too sensitive or "just can't take a joke" when you object. Belittling you or putting down the things you are interested in, being dismissive of you or your likes or dislikes.

Controlling, shaming behaviors. This is often accomplished through threats and monitoring your whereabouts, both digitally and physically. Coming to your work to check up on you. I've heard of people thinking this was caring behavior, when in fact it is a sign of controlling behavior when done obsessively and to check up on whether or not you really are where you said you are going to be. This is not a sign of care, this is a sign of abuse. Lecturing and outbursts, treating you like a child and giving you direct orders rather than treating you as an equal. While acting as if you don't know to do anything on your own, they may also act as if there are certain things they have no idea how to do, so they desperately need you to do it for them.

Accusations, blaming others, or outright denial of things you know to be true. Jealousy, blaming you for their outbursts, lapses in judgment, or any outside problems they may be having. Destroying things and then denying that it happened, despite proof to the contrary. Denying their abuse and possibly claiming that you are the abuser instead. Trivializing your concerns and claiming you have no sense of humor because you have been upset over things they have said in the past.

As the abuse continues, it will lead to emotional neglect and isolation. They will demand respect but not reciprocate. They may shut down communication, prevent you from socializing with others, or dehumanize you when you are the one doing the talking. They may come between you and family members, perhaps even offering what sounds like legitimate reasons for keeping you away from your family. At the same time, they may withhold affection from you, tune you out, or show other signs of indifference to you such as interrupting or disagreeing with you when you say you feel a certain way.

At the end of all this is a state of codependence. When in this state, you may feel as if you deserve this treatment, which is not true, but is hard to accept. You may feel guilty for defending yourself, and even find yourself defending them to other people when they question this behavior. You may even be staying because they claim they cannot live without you.

You may wonder why we are talking so extensively about this sort of abuse in regard to helping yourself access the polyvagal theory of the vagus nerve. The reason is that emotional abuse changes the story you tell yourself and paints your neurological world in a way that you were not designed to see it. Again, this is not your fault. It is a biological function and up until this point, it has helped you survive. However, now you are at the point where you can see the truth, and you can get help. You may need extensive help to see the world in a healthy state again, and that is where the vagus nerve comes in. Begin that pathway to a healthy vagal state even while you are searching for help to get out of an abusive situation. This will help you start to see the world as it is meant to be, and help you gain clarity regarding the path you should follow.

Chapter 7: Potential Dysfunctions

Digestive problem

The vagus nerve is involved from the beginning to the end of the digestion process. It transmits signals from the bacterial of the gut and the cells of the body to the brain, sending information about hunger and craving.

The gut bacterial fill the cravings signal that is transmitted by the vagus nerve with information about nutrients requirements.

The body needs carbohydrate and fat to generate energy, it need protein for the production of amino acids and internal protein. The body also requires other nutrients like vitamins and minerals in smaller quantities.

We ingest most of these nutrients in too while some micronutrients may be ingested as supplements.

The food enters through the mouth and takes a long journey through the entire distance of the digestive tract. The food is digested along the way while the waste products exits at the other end. It takes about 16 to 20 hours for food to digest properly. The time may vary depending on the size, age and gender of the individual. The 16 to 20 hours timeline is believed to be the best.

Anytime below 10 hours is theorized to be too short while anytime more than 24 hour so theorized as too long.

A dysfunction of the vagus nerve can hinder digestion and lead to digestive problems like constipation and diarrhea. These two are mild but common digestion problems.

The biggest problem with digestion being too quick is that the body doesn't have enough time to extract the nutrients in the food. This means that you are wasting the food.

On the other hand, if digestion is too slow, toxins can begin to build-up and bacteria may try to take advantage. It also cause leaky gut.

The digestion of food is an intricate process. After the cells of the body and gut bacteria has transmitted a signal through the vagus nerve to the brain. The brain registers the signal as hunger and we try to find something to eat. As the food sits before us or even through its aroma before it reaches our table the food startles to estimate the salivary glands. It means the body is anticipating the meal. It is waiting and preparing for it. When you ingest the food into your mouth, before swallowing, use your teeth. Chew the food to aid your digestion. The mouth is the grinder of the digestive tract that is why our body evolved to have teeth. Chewing breaks down the food which makes it easier to move and digest them.

Chewing the food also exposes it to the taste buds. The taste buds identify and record the difference nutrients present in the food. They find out if the food contains carbohydrate, protein, and fat. The taste buds use the vagus nerve to transmit this information to the brain.

All the other organs along the digestive tract are signaled by the vagus nerve. This prepares them in anticipation of food. The pancreas, for example generates the required amount of bile and bile salt.

Another impact of chewing is an increase sensation and better enjoyment of the meal. The food tastes better. The taste buds are able to send a more detailed information to the brain. People who chew their food also tend to eat less food than people who swallow food. The chewers are more easily satiated. It also helps that the food will digest better.

Rushing your food and not chewing it are pretty much the same thing. People who do this tend to eat more calories, make poorer dietary choices and they also have low satiety reflex.

The vagus nerves also signals the larynx and pharynx to open the through and let the model of food through. It also triggers the walls of the esophagus to push the food down.

The food then proceeds to the stomach where the stomach acid breaks it down into indigestible fiber and macronutrient. The stomach keeps churning the food before pushing it into the small intestine. The food I'd joined in the small intestine by bile and other enzymes from the liver and gallbladder. This enzymes breakdown the food into simpler compounds. Some of the primary nutrients such as lipids, amino acid and glucose will then be absorbed into the bloodstream.

The macronutrients are then transferred into the liver where they filtered and stored to be supplied to the organs and other parts of the body.

The indigestible fiber cannot be broken down by the enzymes. It is instead moved through the small intestine, to the proximal colon of the large intestine.

The bacterial population of the large intestine then breakdown the fiber to produce minerals, vitamins and precursors for neurotransmitters and hormones. The most active element in digestion is the vagus nerve. It is always working, signaling organ after organ. For optimal functionality the vagus nerve mustn't be dealing with stress during digestion.

Digestion is a linear process. Each organ is signaled by the vagus nerve, it waits for its turn and perform its duty before the food is moved to the next organ. Being active while eating, eating on the go or multitasking while eating adds some stress to the digestive process.

We need to eat in a conducive environment with focus on the food. The vagus nerve won't be able to send the correct signals to the brain if our attention is not on the food. The added street messes with the functionality of the vagus nerve.

Chronical inflammation

When the vagus nerve is not functioning properly, one of the first hints is the inability of the body to properly manage inflammation. It means the vagus nerve is not effectively doing its job, which is to act as a message network between the immune system and the brain. There are many factors that can cause inflammation. That is why experts rarely look at the vagus nerve. Inflammation can be corrected only when we find out what was responsible for it.

Inflammation may be mild and we know that inflammation is the body's way of defending itself. Inflammation really becomes a health problem when it becomes chronic.

Chronic inflammation can manifest itself physically in many ways, from cancer, to auto immune diseases, growth of tumor, and arthritis etc.

Inflammation becomes chronic due to the inability of the vagus nerve to transmit the signals required to stop inflammation. You can try to stimulate the vagus nerve and improve the vagal tone. This improves the vagus nerve's ability to transmit signals between the white blood cells and the brain. Effective signaling from the vagus nerve will reverse inflammation without need for any medication. Then the body can try to repair the damaged cells.

Some of the most common inflammation is caused by physical and emotional trauma so I would like to discuss the relationship between these kinds of inflammation and the vagus nerve. I will also discuss the two main inflammation issues caused by the dysfunctions of the vagus nerve.

Inflammation does not just happen, it is induced by various causes. After all, it is your body's way of reacting to things it finds harmful. Stress puts your body on high alert and enables you to go into a fight-or-flight response whenever you are in danger. However, when your body releases adrenaline, it puts stress in your organs. For example, your heart rate increases and you start sweating or even trembling.

When stress is temporary, stress hormones will definitely come in handy to relieve the situation. But if you are constantly stressed out, the emotional and physical toil on your body becomes too much as your body strives to mitigate all the symptoms of stress.

Inflammation caused by physical and emotional trauma

Physical traumas cause the most obvious types of inflammation. When you sprain an ankle or bump a body part, it soon becomes red, swollen and sore. This is due to the actions of the white blood cells. The cells increase blood flow and secretion to chemicals to the spot in order to repair the damage and fight any invading pathogen. These symptoms are only supposed to exist for a short period of time pending the time that the body heals itself. When they remain it starts to harm the body. It means the cholinergic anti-inflammatory pathway (which acts as a signal network between the antibodies) and the vagus nerve has failed in their task of transmitting information.

There are various reasons for inflammation to remain over a longer than normal period of time. All these reasons prevent the body from healing properly.

One curve ball responsible for inflammation is emotional trauma. This stress applied on the mind can create a negative attitude that affects one's perception of the environment and other people. Emotional trauma may vary in severity and the impact on the individual. The impact of emotional trauma can also be affected by the number of emotionally traumatic event and the how closely together they happen. It is easier for us to recover from things that happened few years apart than for something that happened a few days apart.

Emotionally traumatic events trigger the sympathetic forces that put us in fight or flight mode. This increases the likeliness of inflammation and reduces the ability of the vagus nerve to stop inflammation.

Emotional trauma rarely acts alone. It combines with physical trauma (the quick and ready cause of inflammation) to form a deadly combination. Any inflammation from physical trauma is expanded by the actions of the emotional trauma.

In the end, inflammation becomes chronic and more complicated health problem start to rear their heads. Much like the way chronic stress works, small physical trauma can lead to more complicated health problems, because numerous other emotional and physical trauma have complicated the parasympathetic nerves of the vagus nerve.

Chronic Inflammation of the Gut

The white blood cells can become desensitized to inflammation, if inflammation occurs constantly over a long period of time. These white blood cells are the little soldiers of the body. They protect it. Constant inflammation will impact them negatively.

Inflammation in the gut is a tricky situation because we can't easily identify the symptoms. It doesn't manifest externally until the situation becomes really severe. You can find a test online or visit your health provider.

An imbalance in the microbiome population of the digestive tract is the most common factor responsible for inflammation in the gut. There are other causes such as the consumption of inflammatory food items but the aforementioned one is the most rampant one.

Dysfunctional heart rate

We are told that the average resting human heart rate is between 60 and 100beats per minute. The more calm and collected you are, the lower the heartrate will be, and the more stressed out you are, the faster your heart will beat.

These conditions include Parkinson's disease, sarcoidosis, Crohn's disease, ulcerative colitis, Sjogren's syndrome, amyloidosis, and even chronic inflammatory demyelinating polyneuropathy.

When someone deals with an issue like vasovagal syncope and has relatively common fainting spells, it is often a sign of an immune or metabolic issue that may not yet be diagnosed. Functional lab testing and functional neurology provide insights to the potential underlying root causes of this issue, which is often a symptom of improperly functioning nerves in the autonomic nervous system and hyperactivation of the vagus. Changes in heartrate, blood pressure, and cardiac output that cannot be fully regulated are signs that vagus and the autonomic nervous system are not functioning optimally.

Dysfunctional breathing

The first and most common cause of dysfunctional signaling in the vagus nerve is dysfunctional breathing. Immediately upon exiting our mother's womb, we are tasked with taking our first breath of air. While in the womb, our hearts are already breathing and our digestive tracts are already working thanks to the support of our mothers. Breathing is the first task we are given when we are born, and it's the only thing that our tiny, brand-new bodies have to do to survive outside of the warm, comfortable environment in which we grew and developed for approximately 40 weeks. The doctor or midwife can help us with this initially by clearing our airway, allowing for the free flow of air into the lungs and the contraction and relaxation of our diaphragm muscle. They support this task by clearing fluid that may be obstructing the pathway. This fluid usually enters the airway and lungs when we take some practice breaths very late in our fetal development. The diaphragm must learn to contract and relax, as it is the controlling factor necessary for the act of breathing. The vagus nerve has no effect on the diaphragm. It is controlled by the phrenic nerve, which originates in the neck (from levels 3–5 of the cervical spine) and courses adjacent to the vagus into the thorax and past the lungs and heart before it reaches the most important muscle for the task of breathing. Once our airways are cleared, the task of taking that first breath begins. Our diaphragm contracts and creates a vacuum effect in our thorax, forcing our lungs to expand and take in the external air that contains oxygen, among other gases.

Dysfunctional Airways

Remember the last time you had a stuffy nose? Do you remember trying to breathe in through your nose and feeling terrible? At the same time, your energy was low and you likely had a bit of a sore throat or didn't feel great overall. If your airways are not clear, then it can be very hard to breathe in deeply and fully. This can be a constant issue for someone dealing with a deviated septum, chronic adenoid inflammation, and post-nasal drip. All of these issues can lead to the airways not functioning optimally. Dysfunctional airways are associated with the issue of dysfunctional breathing. When I speak of airways, I am specifically speaking of the nasal passage, the pharynx, the larynx, and the trachea—together, these are known as the upper respiratory tract. The first is dysfunctional posture. We live in the smartphone and laptop age. We sit at our desks and stare at our computer screens for hours on end, then take breaks from our computers to look down at our smartphones. We are all guilty of this, including me. We spend hours in a poor mechanical posture, leading to back and neck pain, then hold our cellphones below our chin. For the most part, we are all aware that postural issues contribute to neck, back, and shoulder pain and mechanical dysfunction of the spine, but it's easy to forget the problems that it causes with airways and the ability to breathe correctly. Here's another test for you to do right now. I want you to sit in a slouched position. Have you done it? Okay, good. Now, I want you to try to take a deep breath in by expanding your belly—breathe with your diaphragm. Was it easy or hard? Most people find it more difficult and possibly even painful to take a deep breath in a slouched position. The reason for this is that the middle portion of the spine (the thoracic spine) is sitting in a flexed forward position when we slouch. To expand and contract optimally, the diaphragm requires a less flexed position of the thoracic spine and an extended position of the lumbar spine.

Dysfunctional sleep

How well do you sleep? Do you wake up feeling rested and full of energy in the morning? When we sleep, we go through five cyclical stages of brain activity. Stages one and two are lighter sleep, often associated with the first 7to 15 minutes of falling asleep. Stages three and four are the deep restorative sleep stages that are associated with muscle and tissue repair, growth and development, boosted immune function, and production of energy for the next day—essentially, all of the tasks mediated by the vagus nerve to help our bodies perform at their best the next day. Vagus nerve activity (measured through heart rate variability) has been shown to be significantly higher during stages three and four of sleep. The fifth stage is rapid-eye movement (REM) sleep. During this phase, heartrate variability decreases. It has been shown that parasympathetic activity significantly decreases during this phase of sleep. Sympathetic activity predominates REM sleep, which is associated with formation of memories as well as dreaming. These phases will take place at different times of the night as we age, but in adulthood, the first four stages are more likely to be cyclical and occur earlier at night, while REM is more common later in sleep.

Chapter8: Illnesses Caused by Stress

Stress causes many kinds of illnesses that involve both the mind and the body.

You may be battling stress and have some of the health issues and diseases listed here:

Insomnia

Lack of sleep and insomnia exacerbates stress. Worry, uncertainty about the future, issues with your job, your relationships, your children, finances keeps a person awake at night. Some people are concerned with caring for a family member who is ill or a death in the family. Just navigating through each day can raise the level of stress. If stress remains uncontrolled, it interferes or delays the ability to fall asleep.

In order to battle against your lack of sleep that is stress-related, there are positive steps that can be taken. Reduce caffeine intake over the course of the day, stop watching TV or surfing on your computer at least an hour before bedtime, shut off all electronics when you're in your bedroom, and do not exercise prior to bedtime. A bedroom that is dimly lit, cool, and comfortable is the type of environment you want to have before you go to sleep.

Shut your mind off from the problems that elevate your stress while getting ready for bed. Instead, think peaceful thoughts, have soothing sounds or music programmed to play for an hour while you drift off to sleep. Prepare your mind for rest.

Violent or disturbing television programs can elevate stress and anxiety, especially in these days of mass shootings and the traumatic aftermath that people experience from these events.

Depression

Stress that remains unresolved can bring up emotions of anger or hopelessness in a person. Both of these emotions can lead to depression and have feelings prolonged.

Feeling chronically unhappy or sad, having trouble thinking with clarity, dealing with loneliness or feeling unloved and uncared for, or feeling shame or guilt, you are probably depressed, which often is related to excessive stress.

Illnesses you may have that are chronic may seem unrelated to depression. However, continuous daily coping with a chronic condition can be stressful and depressing.

A feeling of hopelessness sets in when a chronic condition is a day-to-day battle. The stress of maintaining the condition with medications, routines that can't be ignored, and the never-ending doctor appointments can be a stressful and depressing way to live.

Disordered Eating and Eating Disorders

When you're feeling stressed and overwhelmed with an issue that you just want to have gone away, do you find yourself looking for something to eat, most often that is tasty and sweet when these feelings well up?

Don't feel like you're alone. That's what many people do.

When people are stressed, they usually reach for a carbohydrate-laden food or a sweet treat to get a fast sugar rush. While your blood sugar may elevate for a short period giving you a false sense of energy, it will drop afterward, frequently making you feel sluggish and, sometimes, drowsy and slow.

There is another eating disorder that stress impacts and that is bulimia. Stress is thought to be an initiator for people who suffer from bulimia and end up binge eating.

Chronic stress and stressful events are major causes of eating disorders. Some research has indicated that the overall pressure and stress for bulimics is more than two times greater than it is for normal women.

The stress may be expressed through anger, anxiety or depression, or physical decline and illness.

Try changing your eating habits when you get stressed out. Eat some crisp veggies like carrots or even raw green or red peppers that have a natural sweetness. Cut up an apple and eat a few slices. You can also pop some light butter popcorn. You'll feel fuller with fiber and stay healthy, as well. Don't allow your stress to have you make a bee-line to the cookie jar, your favorite Danish pastry or candy counter.

Panic Attacks and Anxiety

As with depression, disorders linked to anxiety and panic attacks often have a stress-related correlation.

Struggling with issues that cause you to feel ill-at-ease and have you experience extreme stress and that can manifest in fear and nervousness for reasons that are not clear.

Panic attacks and anxiety attacks are usually thought to be interchangeable. However, they are very different. Although they have some similar symptoms, there are differences that are distinct in how they manifest, how they are triggered, the length of time they last and how each is treated.

It is important to understand how different each attack is so your symptoms can be reported to your physician accurately. Their treatment is different.

The onset of an anxiety attack is different, whereas it is a gradual escalation of emotions. It is usually caused by a particular situation that can be targeted as the cause of the attack.

Symptoms of an anxiety attack before it occurs can be the feelings of worry, uneasiness, fearfulness or distress. These feelings usually begin before the actual attack and continue after the attack ends.

An anxiety attack can last longer than 10 minutes. If a certain situation is occurring that has caused the attack, the anxiety will continue until the situation changes or ends.

Panic attacks, on the other hand, come on instantaneously and spontaneously. This attack is instant. There is no gradual escalation, it just comes at any time, no matter what the situation. There is usually no identifiable reason why the attack occurred.

While you're experiencing the attack, you will experience crippling fear, as well as the fear of losing control. You also have a feeling of disassociation from your surroundings, known as derealization. You may also experience a detachment from yourself, known as depersonalization.

Panic attacks last, on average, approximately 10 minutes. After the attack ends, the symptoms dispel after the attack ends (Boring-Bray, 2018).

Physical symptoms for both attacks:

- Nausea

- Lightheadedness and/or dizziness

- Pains in the chest

- Difficulty in breathing

- Sweating

- Throat tightening or choking sensation

- Physical shaking or trembling

- Tingling or numbness

- Headache

If the panic attacks or uncontrolled anxiety attacks persist or accelerate in their occurrence, meeting with a psychologist or a counselor may be a step in the positive direction of dealing with the source of the issue.

Viruses and Colds

Illness of any kind can cause stress, even if the illness may be a common cold or virus. The immune system that is not functioning up -to-par and is being afflicted by stress will often get sick more frequently and quicker.

Alleviating stress can be helpful in regaining your health and healing from illness much faster.

Circulatory problems

Your body's veins and arteries can be made to tighten up due to stress and the response to the fight-or-flight feelings. Blood flow through the body can be compressed and create further problems such as poor circulation, blood clots or even a stroke.

Get a medical checkup and diagnosis about this type of medical issue.

Local or Systemic Infections

Emotional or mental stress can delay or interrupt the physical healing of systemic infections, like food poisoning or local infections such as an infected toe/toenail or a splinter that goes unattended.

The body's positive energy is drained due to stress as it attempts to deal with worrying about stress-related problems. There isn't much left by way of energy to sustain the immune functions of the body to heal infectious injuries and illnesses.

Diabetes

Blood sugar that is out of control that is caused by stress is common in those who have diabetes. People diagnosed with diabetes need to eat and maintain a lifestyle that has to regulate their blood sugar levels in prescribed limits. Sugar levels increase or decrease based on the amount of stress a person with this disease is under.

Diabetics who are overwhelmed and stressed need to monitor their blood sugar levels. If they're on mediation for type 2 diabetes, they need to take their medication, while type 1 diabetics need to monitor their insulin intake. Eating properly is also key to maintaining blood sugar levels.

Heart Problems

Your heart can palpitate, increase the pulse rate and have your blood pressure increase when you are stressed. Stress can put tremendous pressure on the heart and can damage it. Your blood cholesterol can increase by elevated stress levels. Monitor your blood pressure if you are under consistent stress to avert possible strain on the heart.

Exercise and proper eating habits can also help in reducing the stress levels that can affect your heart.

Cancer

Stress that is prolonged can cause chronic inflammation that contributes to cancer risk and exacerbates an already cancerous condition.

Although stress doesn't necessarily cause cancer in itself, all the other health problems that are linked with stress can cause the manifestation of cancer.

Overeating, smoking, and drinking alcohol in excess all can elevate the risk of developing cancer. These habits can develop and be stress-related.

Studies have shown that there are links between certain types of cancers and stress. The body's immune system is suppressed by stress; a person who is battling ongoing stress may not be able to fight against a major illness like cancer.

Other studies indicate that the recurrence of cancer can be affected by stress and fear of cancer returning. The production of the hormone cortisol occurs when the body is stressed for a period of time. This can inhibit the immune system of the body and make it more prone to the recurrence of cancer. (University of Rochester Medical Center, 2007)

New homeopathic treatments such as musical and relaxation therapy are now being included along with the medical treatments for cancer patients. These treatments can help to lessen and ward off the stress that the disease creates and reduce the side effects of the medical treatments prescribed that can be physically overwhelming.

Post-Traumatic Stress Disorder (PTSD)

This disorder develops in those who have had a trauma either directly or indirectly affect them. They suffer from functional impairment or distress for a period of time, usually a month at minimum and some who have been exposed to extreme trauma for the remainder of their lives.

The symptoms of PTSD include experiencing the traumatic again, evading reminders of the trauma, elevated anxiety and negative feelings or thoughts. Mass shootings, natural disasters, terrorist attacks and cities that are under siege have added to the burden of PTSD. Now global in scope and affects 4-6% of the world's populations, the major portion of traumas are associated with sexual or physical violence and accidents.

There is no known cure for PTSD and the treatments that are currently used to help those who suffer from trauma are not effective for all patients.

There is evidence that Vagus nerve stimulation (VNS) may be an aid that is beneficial when added to other exposure-based therapies. The Vagus nerve serves as a connection to the brain from the peripheral autonomic nervous system.

It communicates with the brain and sends a signal at times when heightened sympathetic activity is activated. The Vagus nerve counteracts the sympathetic nerve response. (McIntyre, 2018)

In many ways, stress can be more difficult to deal with and harder on the body than physical work. If you are under chronic stress, you may be at risk of contracting one of these illnesses. If you are feeling any of these symptoms, schedule an appointment to see a physician and have a physical workup and evaluation.

Hair Loss

Stress and loss of hair can be related. Although there it is common for hair to change in thickness and texture over our life. However, if you're the one who is stressing about the hair you're losing, this news is not so good and the stressing about losing or thinning of your hair is probably one of the reasons the hair loss is happening.

If your hair is thinning or being lost because of stress, here is some information for you to take away with you to understand why hair loss happens under chronic, stressful circumstances.

Hair loss caused by stress can be controlled if the stress is managed. Emotional and physical stress that is excessive, like that connected with surgery, illness, or injury causes hair loss (Scott, 2019).

Other causes of hair loss are:

- Hormonal changes

- Pregnancy, childbirth and birth control

- Chemotherapy

- Innate nervous habits

Relieving Stress

Stress is an occurrence that at times can't be avoided, but knowing how to manage and minimize it can help in preventing hair loss. When there is a reduction of stress in some areas, you'll have more stamina to contain any stress that can't be evaded.

Reversing your stress "reaction" at the moment can minimalize the experience of chronic stress. Having a stress management plan and methods that can act rapidly is important. Breathing exercises are a fast and simple way to cope and manage stress.

Vagus Nerve Effect on Stress

The Vagus nerve can relieve stress and anxiety by regulating your relaxation response and counteracting the sympathetic nervous system response.

It can be empowering to better understand how our nervous system functions and what we can do to calm it down when we need to.

Although the most interesting of what is known of the anxiety and the effect the Vagus nerve has is that it also sends feelings we have of calm, anger, relaxation, or nervousness and sends it to the brain.

The sympathetic nervous system feeds hormones like cortisol and adrenaline to prepare us for action. The intervention of the Vagus nerve intercedes and brings in relaxation and rest to the body.

The sympathetic nerve works like an accelerator and stimulates us, while we experience a slower, more relaxed pace and bring balance to the body through the parasympathetic nervous system, which decreases the blood pressure and heart rate.

All this reduction can ease the stress and anxiety that stems from the sympathetic nervous system. When stressful situations occur, it is this nervous system that is stimulated. We don't have the ability to turn off the physiological response; there isn't much more time before problems manifest as the stress and tension continue.

As stated earlier, the brain reacts to stress and anxiety by increasing the production of hormones.

This, in turn, activates adrenaline and cortisol. These hormones act to suppress the immune system and cause inflammation. We become ill more easily when we are stressed, anxious, or depressed.

Chapter9: The Polyvagal Theory And PTSD

PTSD, or post-traumatic stress disorder, has gained considerable attention in recent years due to its occurrence among military veterans, especially those returning from the long, ongoing conflicts in the Middle East. These traumatized individuals may have experienced severe physical injuries, but in many cases, however, their injuries are psychological, resulting from their overwhelming reactions to their battlefield experiences. In earlier wars, mentally traumatized veterans were said to be suffering from shell shock, the result of seeing and feeling the consequences of war. We now recognize this condition as PTSD.

Typical symptoms of PTSD include flashbacks of the traumatic event or the inability to stop thinking about it obsessively, anxiety, depression, sleeplessness and recurring nightmares. Beyond the discomforts of experiencing PTSD, it is now known that it can lead to suicidal thoughts and suicidal behavior. In many cases, PTSD can lead to continuing deep depression and anxiety, as well as eating disorders, and substance abuse, notably drugs and alcohol.

Apart from veterans, people in all walks of life may have had terrifying, traumatic experiences, either themselves or as witnesses, that trigger PTSD, like an automobile accident, sexual or other physical assault, a serious fall at home, or loss of a loved one. Any of these extremely distressing experiences may initiate the PTSD response. Previously, victims of PTSD may have been told to shape up or get over it, but today, PTSD is a recognized, serious psychological condition requiring professional assistance to resolve. It may affect children as well as adults.

Based on the Polyvagal Theory, it is now believed by many psychologists that PTSD has its roots in the dorsal vagal response of the parasympathetic nervous system. This is the primitive freezing, or shutting down mechanism that is triggered when the person or animal faces an insurmountable or overwhelming immediate threat. When this dorsal vagal response is initiated, it can cause immobility, speechlessness, fainting and even severe shock. PTSD appears to be an ongoing form of dorsal vagal reaction.

Before reviewing the Polyvagal Theory's potential treatments for overcoming dorsal vagal-caused PTSD, an understanding of the human brain's evolution and functions is presented for perspective.

The Three-Part Brain

The human brain, with its complexity of 100 billion or so neurons and perhaps 100 trillion neural connections, is generally known to be organized into two hemispheres, the left, recognized for controlling rational, logical, organizational thoughts, and the right, associated with creative, imaginative and unstructured thinking. We also know that the functioning nervous system is comprised of the brain, spinal cord, and between them, the brainstem.

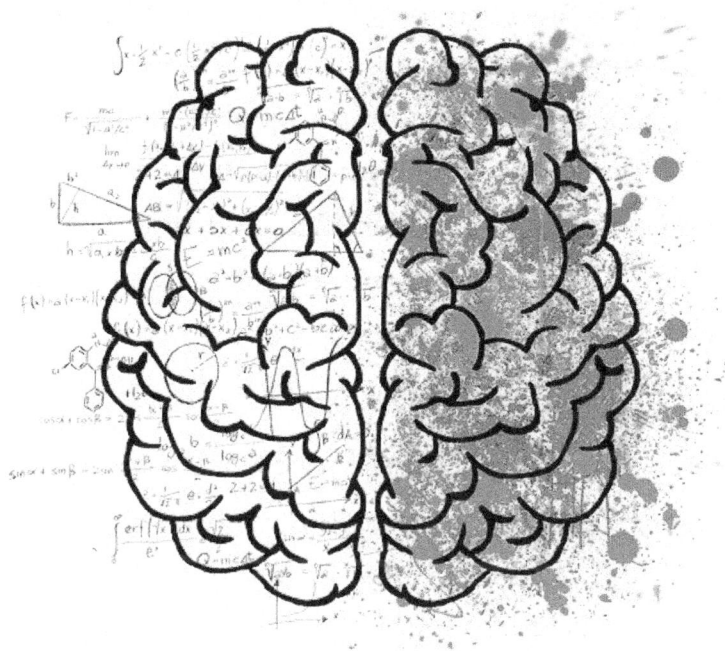

The brain is where all the conscious and unconscious action takes place, from managing our cardiovascular, respiratory and digestive functions to feelings, senses and sensations, and embracing all thought, memory and decision-making.

The spinal cord is the central cable that receives all nerve impulses from the extremities and forwards these impulses to the brain, and returns the brain's reactions to the impulses with the appropriate reaction.

The brainstem is where 10 of the 12 cranial nerves originate and extend to the organs and other key areas, including number 10, the longest, most diverse neuron, the vagus nerve.

But we know today that the evolution of the human brain has been built upon a sequential three-part structure, beginning with the earliest, most primitive part, called the reptilian brain, then continuing to evolve an early old or paleomammalian brain, and concluding with a more sophisticated new or neo-mammalian brain. This concept of a three-part evolution-driven brain structure was identified first in the 1960's by a neuroscientist, Dr. Paul MaLean, who called it the triune brain, and postulated that these three parts of the brain still struggle to coexist. Each part has specific functions to perform:

The early, reptilian brain, is responsible for basic, involuntary reflex actions, including reproduction urges, arousal to a range of stimuli and maintaining a balanced, normal state, or homeostasis. It can be considered a fundamental survival mechanism. One of its continuing characteristics is compulsiveness.

The old-mammalian, or paleomammalian brain, is positioned to surround the reptilian brain, it manages emotions, learning and memory functions. It enabled early mammals to remember and act upon favorable and unfavorable experiences, for example.

The new-mammalian, or neo-mammalian brain is responsible for conscious thought and self-awareness, and is positioned atop the two early brain parts. All of our reasoning, decision-making and rationalizations occur here.

But one may ask if we really evolved from reptiles? The concept of our brains evolving from reptiles comes as a surprise. We understand that we evolved from mammals, since we ourselves are mammals. Okay, but reptiles? Over the long course of evolution, the earliest mammals evolved from, yes, reptiles, and not from the dinosaurs that became extinct 66 million years ago, or the dinosaurs that grew feathers and evolved into birds. Our reptilian ancestors were small, and obviously smarter than the large dinosaurs, which gave them an edge in natural selection. They had strong survival skills built into their small but highly functional reptilian brains, and some of these hardy reptiles evolved into small mammals. In their turn, these early mammals evolved more complex brains, the paleomammalian brain, with its added values of learning, memory and emotion. Still later, as mammals further evolved as primates, the third neo-mammalian brain component developed, giving Homo Sapiens the ability to think consciously and with increasing complexity.

The three parts of our current triune brain correspond, approximately, to the brainstem and cerebellum (reptilian), limbic brain, which includes the hippocampus, amygdala, and hypothalamus (paleomammalian) and the neocortex (neo-mammalian). Because the reptilian-originated brainstem reacts completely unconsciously and immediately for survival, historically, it tends to dominate in many situations, when the brain perceives a danger or other need for prompt action. The conflict between the purely instinctive reptilian brain and the two more advanced components is considered by some to be represented by Freud's ongoing battles between the conscious and the subconscious.

These aspects include the two-hemisphere structure, vertical networks connecting the layers and departments of the brain, and a near infinite number of interacting neurons, as well as variations in brain structure due to gender, genetic and environmental influences.

In recent times, the precise sequential evolution and functioning of the triune brain, and its exclusivity among humans have been questioned by some animal behaviorists, since complex brains have developed among non-mammal species, including certain birds. Also, new studies demonstrate that in humans, the prefrontal cortex performs complex functions that are apart from the functions of the neocortex.

Post-Traumatic Brain Reeducation

Separate from the psychological disorders associated with PTSD, there are physical brain injuries resulting in serious trauma. About 10 million people worldwide suffer traumatic brain injury (TBI) each year, and many cases are fatal, and most who survive the injury experience some degree of cognitive impairment. These trauma may occur in any number of circumstances, including vehicular accidents, sports injuries, falls inside and outside the home, acts of conflict or violence, even being struck by falling objects.

There are a range of treatments to reverse the impairment, and the type and duration of treatment depends on the type and severity of the trauma. Generally, a multidisciplinary set of treatments is required, involving the psychiatric and neurologic medical practices, as well as pharmacotherapy.

Classifying TBI as mild, moderate or severe depends on several key factors: Degree of post-traumatic consciousness, duration of the coma, if experienced by the patient, and the degree and duration of post-traumatic amnesia. Generally, TBI patients whose symptoms continue for one month or more are classified as either moderate or severe, and whose full recovery make takes years, while those showing marked improvement within a few weeks are considered to be mild cases and often return to full cognitive function within two months.

There are a number of impairments to the cognitive functions following TBI. These are the most commonly treated:

• Decreased ability to concentrate

• Impaired attentiveness

- Reduced visual spatial cognizance

- Tendency to be easily distracted

- Memory lapses and impairments

- Loss of executive ability (decision-making)

- Disrupted communications skills

- Judgmental lapses and dysfunctions

Reeducation of TBI patients begins with assessments based on standardized testing protocols, including visual and auditory attentiveness, visual and verbal measurements, language comprehension and understanding, executive function (decisiveness), overall mental and intellectual function and motor function.

Post-traumatic brain reeducation is undertaken primarily through cognitive rehabilitation, which works to increase the injured person's abilities in the processing and interpretation of information, and the overall performance of mental functions. Cognitive rehabilitation is mostly effective in mild or moderate levels of TBI and with persons who have a high level of motivation to succeed in the recovery. The multidisciplinary group that collaborates on brain reeducational therapy may include doctors, speech and language specialists, physical and occupational therapists, among others. However, it is recognized that each patient's treatment will be unique, prescribed and tailored to each individual, based on the specific injuries suffered and resultant trauma.

One important approach that has wide application is attention process training (ATP), which is based on mental skills training, gradually increasing the complexity of the exercises, from simple initially, and subsequently increasing in complexity, forcing the brain to retrain itself. The exercises include selective attention, focused attentiveness, alternating attention, divided attentiveness and sustained attentiveness.

The Parasympathetic Recovery

The Polyvagal Theory links PTSD to one dimension of the parasympathetic nervous system (PNS), the early-evolved dorsal vagal freeze survival mechanism. The dorsal vagal mechanism may protect an animal by allowing it to play dead until the coast is clear, but in a human being, it can lead to inaction, inability to think or speak, or worse, passing out or fainting, shock or even cardiac arrest. With the linking of PTSD to the dorsal vagal mechanism, a previously unrecognized cause may now be open to evaluation and potentially, to alleviate the symptoms of PTSD.

Specifically, the other, more recently evolved PNS response, the calming, relaxing, socially engaging ventral vagal response may be applied to reduce the emotional and physical symptoms of PTSD. Now the methods used to achieve vagal tone and lower heart rates and breathing rates, reactivate the digestive system and induce an all-encompassing state of calm and relaxation may be applied by the individual, easily, every day. The practice of deep, slow breathing, with forceful extension of the diaphragm to tone the vagus nerve, is applicable as part of meditation or Yoga, or simply done without other techniques.

It can also include auricular and facial massage, massage of the vagus nerve as it passes next to the right and left carotid artery in the neck, and cold facial therapy. The practice of mindfulness, or being in the moment, in which all outside thoughts are prevented from intruding, can also be beneficial, as the person concentrates on every external sound, every feeling, every awareness of things in the environment. Vocal stimulation of the vagus nerve can be done easily by singing, gargling, or reciting a mantra while performing mantra and transcendental meditation.

Another application of Polyvagal Theory to treating PTSD is for the individual to recognize that the symptoms of PTSD are biological in nature, caused by the body's primitive instincts and reflexes to protect itself, and that the body can be taught to relax, get over it, rejoin and socially engage with those who are living active, normal lifestyles. This is called somatic awareness, and it trains the individual to become aware of basic bodily functions like heart rate and breathing, and to consciously try to slow them down. The deep breathing exercises may be helpful in achieving a sense of bodily control.

The reduction or elimination of PTSD symptoms can further be achieved by practicing a series of mental exercises called attentional control, a conscious effort to recognize the cues that may trigger PTSD reactions, and gently but firmly cancel them out by acknowledging that there is no danger, nothing to fear, and all is well. This form of body awareness is called cognitive behavior therapy (CBT), and it encourages the individual to be aware that an unneeded fight or flight response is continuing and can be shut down by conscious thought, replacing disturbing thoughts and memories with relaxing, peaceful thoughts. Over time and with practice, the replacement of bad thoughts with positive ones will make the cooling down of the dorsal vagal action-orientation easier.

Reading Body Language

Body language has long been associated with a few popular positions and movements that are believed to be subconscious cues as to a person's true meaning or intentions. For example, having one's arms crossed signals a negative interest in what is being said, or a hand over one's mouth while speaking may be a sign of a lie being told. Unconsciously nodding one's head indicates agreement, a handshake suggests type of character, depending on whether it is firm or weak, and if eye contact is maintained or not. In reality, most of these body language cues are anecdotal and may have some basis, or they may not.

But Polyvagal Theory has shed a new light on body language, on multiple levels, by revealing one's interest in a social engagement, for example, or sending a signal that can trigger social engagement or other interaction in the second person, who may, in turn, respond with their own body language subconsciously. The use of facial expressions to elicit various types of responses is being used to communicate and engage with autistic children, in testimony to the effectiveness of this approach.

Do the popular body language signals really mean anything, or are they, as implied above, merely anecdotal, believed and circulated but without substantiation? A study conducted by UCLA found that only 7% of what is said is actually believed or acknowledged, based only on the words spoken. The tonality of the speaker's voice accounts for 38% of communications, leaving 50% of communications being based on body language, gestures and expressions.

Resistance to what is being said or shown is frequently shown by crossed arms and crossed legs.

A smile is not sincere when it is limited to the mouth, whereas a sincere smile engages more of the face, including crinkling the eyes.

Mirroring or imitating your own body positions is a sign that the other person is in agreement with what you are saying or proposing.

Power positions radiate a sense of command or control. A person who assumes control will tend to stand upright, extend arms and otherwise occupy more space in a room. This type of person is encouraging interaction or possibly engagement.

Eye contact is not always synonymous with engagement or interest because extended or prolonged eye contact may be forced or deliberate, suggesting the person is hiding a true intention.

Discomfort or surprise may cause raised eyebrows. Conversely, a truly interested person will not tend to raise their eyebrows when spoken to, except to acknowledge an exceptionally unusual remark.

Nodding is positive, except when it's exaggerated because too much nodding suggests discomfort with what is being said.

Tension signals stress. A furrowed brow, tightened neck muscles or a clenched jaw may be signs that what is being said is making the person uncomfortable.

Are these findings valid? Probably to some degree, but it's important to realize that the subject of body language has been widely debated for decades. As a result, many people you may be speaking with, or meet in an interview, may be consciously nodding or smiling or firmly shaking your hand, deliberately trying to make a good impression. You, in turn, might consider your own body language, and try not to send the wrong message.

The Polyvagal Theory

And Emotional Stress

Emotional reactions can trigger not one but two physical responses: the well-known defensive call to action of the sympathetic nervous system, and the more primal dorsal vagal response that can freeze and immobilize a person. Physical actions, conversely, like Yoga, meditation, managed breathing and massages can tone the vagus nerve, triggering the calming, relaxing emotions of the parasympathetic nervous system (also called the ventral vagal response), and its enablement of social engagement.

Chapter 10:   Power of Your Body

Exercise

Exercise is a necessary part of healing from chronic pain. You don't have to become an active bodybuilder or an athlete, but some degree of body movement is highly desirable to prevent chronic pain. Body movements release the "stuck" energy in our body and ensure a smooth flow of energy to prevent any pain.

Exercising is a great way to reduce your anxiety. Whether you wake up earlier in the morning before you have to go to work and go for a run, or if you can go when you get home from and jog around the block.

Also, if you do exercise more this will help with your self-esteem. Exercising will make you healthier and you will feel better about yourself. If you are worried about your health and it is making your anxiety worse, get out there and do some exercises. You don't even have to leave your house; you could just find an exercise DVD and start doing some exercise from your own living room. To really help lower anxiety, it is a good idea that each time you exercise to be sure it is for 30 minutes or more. Studies have shown that it takes about thirty minutes for your anxiety to lower when exercising.

If you don't want to exercise alone, grab a friend to do this activity with you. This will make you happy and you can have someone to talk to about the things you are anxious about. It's great to have someone who you can let all of your feelings be expressed to who can help you. Healthy exercise has some surprising implications for those with anxiety disorders and other psychological conditions including depression. The mechanisms by which exercise and mental health are related are not fully understood, but many medical experts around the world now acknowledge that exercise has a major impact on a wide range of psychological conditions. It is even now believed that exercise can be as effective at combating depression as many commonly prescribed drugs.

Short bursts of activity a few times a day are the type of exercise that experts recommend. A brisk walk lasting only ten minutes is believed to be enough to raise your emotional state for a couple of hours. For those with anxiety disorders, it can be hard to get out and about on occasion. For some, with severe conditions, it can seem impossible. Exercise, however, will really help to improve your emotional state and take your mind off anxiety. Use the following tips to increase your chances of successfully incorporating exercise into your life.

Moderate level intensity exercise is recommended as perfect for improving your physical health and also your mental health. This includes; walking briskly, cycling, jogging or swimming. Walking and jogging should not need any investment and if you're uncomfortable alone, partner up with a friend or relative.

Ideally buddy up with someone who is addressing the same issues or has a good understanding of them, for extra support.

When we exercise, the brain releases endorphins, or "feel good" chemicals that are responsible for the "high" that many people feel during and after exercise. Another benefit of exercise for those with depression is that it lends purpose and structure to each day. Outdoor exercise has been shown to be especially effective for lifting mood.

Regular exercise can help maintain a healthy weight, which can be a problem in depressed people. Exercise promotes overall wellbeing, including heart health and a toned, more muscular body. The weight-bearing aspects of exercise prevent the body from losing bone mass and decrease the risk of osteoporosis, a particular benefit for women.

People who suffer from anxiety may not be interested in exercise. When someone is overwhelmed by the stress of everyday life, working out seems less than appealing. However, research shows that exercise plays an important role in reducing anxiety symptoms.

While exercise has been clinically proven to reduce anxiety and improve mood, it can also treat a number of other health problems. Health issues can be a major anxiety trigger, and easing the symptoms of those ailments can reduce anxiety symptoms further.

In addition, exercising can help people relax. When a person exercises, their body releases hormones that produce a calming effect. Exercise also increases body temperature, which can be very relaxing. Working up a sweat is tiring, but it's a great way to calm down.

Speed Walking

Speed walking, more often referred to as power walking or race walking, is a technique of walking at a rapid pace. Walking is a great alternative to running and is oftentimes much easier and more accessible to a greater variety of people. Walking provides all of the aerobic benefits of running while steering clear of many of the injuries associated with high-impact techniques of running. The activity of walking at an increased rate then walking "normally" can help participants lose weight, tone their muscles, and also increase their mood.

Not only is speed walking valuable for the muscles and joints, but it also reinforces overall health.

Stretching

Stretching is something everyone should do on a regular basis, and those with chronic back pain will benefit most from stretching the soft the muscles, ligaments, and tendons in and around the spine.

It is a fact that when motion is limited the back becomes stiff, which can result in more pain. Those who suffer from chronic back pain need to stretch regularly and perform appropriate stretching movements to benefit from the sustained and long-term relief from the increased motion.

One top recommendation for dealing with chronic pain is by getting regular exercise. Exercise will help with different types of pain - from helping with arthritis by getting your body moving, to boosting your mood, when you have pain from Crohn's disease or fibromyalgia.

Yoga for Chronic Pain

Yoga can be defined as a practice based on harmonizing the mind, body, and soul. By practicing Yoga every day, you will not only explore your true self or your inner self, but also develop the feeling that you are one with nature and environment. Yoga aids the overall well-being of the body and focuses mainly on developing relationship with the natural world around us.

Pain is not just influenced by physical injury or illness, it is also greatly affected by our thoughts, anxiety, trauma, stress and emotions. Stress and pain are closely interrelated - you may experience pain when stressed and stress can also increase the intensity of the pain. When there is increased stress, your breathing becomes heavier, erratic and ragged. Your mood is also altered along with some tension and tightening of the muscles. These symptoms of chronic pain can even increase the toxins in the body and decrease oxygen levels.

Yoga addresses these problems effectively, as it involves the techniques of deep breathing and meditation, which helps in the absorption of much-needed oxygen and also in the relaxation of mind and body. These breathing techniques ensure that the muscles of the lungs, diaphragm, back, and abdomen are fully utilized. When the muscles are loose and relaxed, they can help in releasing the built-up tension in the body and facilitate proper flow of energy throughout. Stress and anxiety levels will also be reduced gradually.

Yoga, or simple stretching, are simple practices that should be applied to everyday life to reduce the tension of stress and keep the muscles in proper working order. There are specific stretches that can focus on problem areas such as the neck or lower back. These stretches can be assigned from a personal trainer, massage therapist, or physiotherapist. Yoga can be enjoyed at home or in a studio with several other participants. There are many forms of yoga ranging from hatha yoga to hot yoga. The focus in yoga is on breath control, meditation, stretching, and balance. Not all forms of yoga are spiritual with chants and mantras, if you don't feel comfortable with that form of practice.

Exercise in general is good for chronic pain, but specific exercises, especially certain yoga positions, help to decrease some types of pain, like shoulder or neck pain.

Additionally, the relaxation techniques you will learn, can teach you how to manage the different types of chronic pain more effectively.

If you are considering trying yoga techniques for your chronic pain, you need to consider the style of yoga you will do.

While all forms of yoga can be beneficial for your body, mind and spirit, certain exercises are actually directed towards people who are struggling with chronic pain.

There are multiple yoga poses or asanas and different stance can be used. Individuals with chronic pain should begin with a slow-paced, gentle yoga pose. Benefits of yoga include improved ability to handle stress, feeling more relaxed throughout the day and improvements in sleep quality. Studies have proven that yoga is helpful to prevent fibromyalgia, among other chronic pain conditions.

Massage Therapy

Massage therapy has become overwhelmingly popular, and rightfully so; in addition to feeling good, it has a number of health benefits. Massage therapy is wonderful for any type of pain, be it chronic, acute or simply from fatigue, work, and tension. There are various massage therapies available to meet all types of needs, including Shiatsu, Swedish, hot oil and deep tissue.

Massage has also been used as a natural anxiety remedy for ages; it may be as simple as rubbing your neck gently but whichever the case you are massaging it is an effective way to calm your nerves. The benefits of any massage therapy are many, including stress relief, relaxation, lowered blood pressure, lowered tension in the muscles, and it also improves deeper breathing. As the book unfolds, I will discuss therapeutic massage as a natural remedy for anxiety disorders, in this case it will be a deep and precise tool.

A skilled and trained massage therapist will know exactly what to do once the pain problem is explained. Massage also does wonders for fatigue and stress, both of which are known to increase pain and go hand in hand with arthritis and other chronic pain conditions. It can also help to calm anxiety, which often afflicts those who suffer from chronic pain.

If you can afford it, get a massage regularly - weekly or even twice per week. Physical therapists and chiropractors also offer therapeutic massage, so it may be covered under medical insurance.

There are also electronic massagers on the market that are great options. These include mobile units, which are spot massage products that target the neck or specific areas. There are also strap onto chair units that offer shiatsu for the entire back, many come with a heat option.

The most significant health benefit of massage is that it provides the sensation of touch, which is critical in both early childhood development and overall adult health. Levels of somatotropin, or human growth hormone, correlate directly with the amount of physical contact you receive.

Massage also cues relaxation in your nervous system. One of the biggest benefits of massage is that it feels great, especially if you're in pain. Nerves that carry information about the sensation of touch to the brain are more heavily myelinated than the nerves that carry information about pain, so touch information travels faster than pain information. This is why you instinctively rub the skin around a painful area; the touch sensation temporarily drowns out the pain sensation, and you're given a brief moment of relief.

Massage also feels good because it temporarily reduces muscle tension. Pressing on tight muscles lengthens them in the same way that gentle prolonged static stretching does, and after an hour or so of this manual lengthening you may stand up feeling like your muscles are made of jelly. If your massage therapist applies a great deal of pressure, your stretch reflex may be activated immediately, making you feel tight and sore soon after a massage. A good rule of thumb is that if you feel pain during a massage, you're probably going to feel some soreness afterward as well. While it can be difficult or awkward in the moment, it's better to ask your massage therapist to press more gently than to suffer the consequences. It is absolutely not necessary to apply a painful amount of pressure to reap the benefits of a massage. Moreover, if you're in pain, a deep massage can increase and prolong your pain by making your muscles tighter.

Lastly, massage temporarily softens connective tissues, which increases flexibility and range of motion. Tendons, ligaments, fascia (which surrounds, supports, and separates structures of the body), and scar tissue (which forms to heal an injury) are all made of collagen fibers arranged in varying patterns and densities. As muscles become habitually tighter and movement decreases, connective tissues also respond by tightening. Movement and heat can make these collagen structures more flexible and fluid.

For people with chronic pain, the most beneficial aspect of massage may be that it lowers stress, thereby reducing the sensation of pain and reactivity of the nervous system. However, a massage by itself is not enough to change deeply learned habitual movements or your resting level of muscle tension. The sensory awareness that can be gained through massage is valuable, but if it isn't followed by actual motor education in the form of voluntary movement, little lasting progress will be made. You must actively retrain your nervous system, and you can't do that with massage alone.

Brain Balance

First, you have to make sure your brain is balanced. Without a balanced nervous system, your efforts to eliminate chronic pain will be wasted. Many things can cause brain imbalances. Most common are head injuries and exposure to electromagnetic radiation from personal wireless devices. Things that increase brain imbalance risk factors include:

• Using Bluetooth devices and cell phones, walkie talkies, using desktop and laptop computers and iPads.

• Eating processed foods that have MSG.

• Consuming drinks containing artificial sweeteners, and drinking fluoridated water.

• Leading a stressful life.

• Not getting enough quality sleep.

Chapter11:   Body and Mind Control Connection

People who have great enthusiastic wellbeing know about their musings, sentiments, and practices. They have learned healthy approaches to adapt to the pressure and issues that are a typical piece of life. They like themselves and have sound connections.

In any case, numerous things that occur in your life can disturb your passionate wellbeing. These can prompt healthy sentiments of pity, stress, or tension. Indeed, even great or needed changes can be as upsetting as undesirable changes. These things include:

- Being laid off from your activity

- Having a kid leave or get back

- Dealing with the demise of a friend or family member

- Getting separated or wedded

- Suffering a disease or damage

- Getting occupation advancement

- Experiencing cash issues

- Moving to another home

- Having or embracing a child.

Your body reacts to the manner in which you think, feel, and act. This is one sort of "mind/body connection." When you are focused on, on edge, or upset, your body responds in a way that may reveal to you that something isn't right. For instance, you may grow hypertension or a stomach ulcer after an, especially distressing occasion, for example, the passing of a friend or family member.

Way to Improved Health

There are ways that you can improve your passionate wellbeing. Initially, attempt to perceive your feelings and comprehend why you are having them. Sifting through the reasons for bitterness, stress, and uneasiness in your life can assist you with dealing with your passionate wellbeing. The following are some other supportive tips.

Discover some stunning realities about the mind-body connection:

We as a whole have the Mind-Body Connection

Regardless of whether intentionally mindful of it or not, every one of us encounters the mind-body connection regularly of our lives. Rather than thinking about the connection as something out of sight reach, or something just realistic through long stretches of yoga and reflection, recollect it is constantly here. Mouth-watering over a tasty looking sweet, or anxious "butterflies" in the stomach before making an introduction, or running a race, are on the whole ideal instances of characteristic personality body connections, which a large portion of us have encountered eventually. Once in a while, the mind-body connection can deliver negative results, such as neglecting to meet athletic, scholastic, or expert objectives because of dread made by the brain.

Our Bodies React to How We Think

All that we are emerges with our contemplations. With our musings, we make the world.

Buddha

As such, on the off chance that we are continually thinking negative, reckless considerations, our bodies will go with the same pattern. Enthusiastic and mental lopsidedness can begin as something like pressure incited cerebral pains, tight shoulders, and an irritated upper back, and lead to unfortunate weight increase or misfortune, a sleeping disorder, and hypertension. Then again, we can put forth a cognizant attempt to think all the more decidedly and to create healthy ways of dealing with stress forever's pressure and preliminaries. After some time, the condition of our passionate and psychological well-being can be harmed or help the body's resistant framework.

We Can Make Ourselves Sick & We Can Make Ourselves Well

Studies show our ways of dealing with stress and ways we handle pressure straightforwardly associate to how we manage genuine ailments, including malignant growth. Ceaseless pressure influences the body in a negative manner, and over significant stretches of time, long haul pressure can make us increasingly vulnerable to diabetes, hypertension, heart illnesses, and a few diseases.

Notwithstanding, by utilizing our intrinsic personality body connection in a constructive manner, by keeping our brains and bodies fit as a fiddle with exercise and nourishment, we can keep feelings of anxiety lower. At the end of the day, the better we can adapt by remaining quiet and decreasing mental pressure, we will thusly lessen physical worry, alongside the possibility of building up a sickness.

We Also Have a BODY-Mind Connection

In the event that we focus, it is anything but difficult to see the effect the body has on our perspective also. For instance, when ladies' bodies are getting ready for monthly cycle, it is the hormones inside the body causing the entirety of the feared indications (cramps, swelling, weakness, enthusiastic awkwardness, and so forth.). Another case of body-mind responses is this season's cold virus. More than likely, an individual begins to feel unwell intellectually the day or a couple of days before the body uncovered the irritated throat, nasal clog, and other basic physical manifestations.

On the other side, the body-mind connection is inconceivably positive, regardless of whether it is endorphins created after exercise or stress alleviation during a back rub. In the physical stances of yoga, it is imagined that specific stances produce certain psychological states. Backbends, for instance, are thought to animate the psyche, while reversals may expedite a calmer state. Exercise can be a modest method to help our center, states of mind, and by and large wellbeing.

Nourishment Affects Both Our Bodies and Minds

It returns to that familiar adage, "We are what we eat." Every single piece or fluid going through our lips has a type of impact on our minds. Our wholesome admission, consistently, can have immense effects both negative and positive on how we feel, on account of the substance serotonin. Basically, when serotonin levels are high, we're more joyful, and when they're low, we become discouraged.

Eating such a large number of carbs and sugar can diminish affectability to serotonin, which prompts awful states of mind, and in the long run stoutness. To adjust serotonin levels, eating protein can be the arrangement, particularly before carb-admission. Rather than gobbling a sugary jolt of energy noontime, go for a nibble high in protein to keep the temperament positive and vitality up, maintaining a strategic distance from an accident later.

Standard Sleep Is a Must for Mind & Body

Besides nourishment and exercise, rest likewise assumes a tremendous job in keeping up sound serotonin levels and keeping our brains and bodies content with one another. Serotonin's essential activity in the body is to quiet, along these lines, it is intently attached to how vitality is - or isn't - used (for example exercise and rest). Without rest, our cerebrums can be contrarily influenced, by disturbing our mind's reaction to serotonin. At the end of the day, it is essential to keep up a predictable resting design, so as to keep the psyche and body healthy.

Reflection Can Help Our Hearts

As indicated by the American Heart Connection, medicinal proof uncovers a certifiable complementary connection between the brain and body. Practices like reflection and other unwinding strategies have appeared to change mind-body yet in addition mind-heart connections. While there is a shortage of concentrates legitimately tending to how mind-heart intercessions can help patients with the congestive cardiovascular breakdown, the AHA closed reflection could help with tension and wretchedness, which regularly match with the genuine disease.

Pondering for around 15 minutes every day can likewise help any individual who needs to remain focused and quiet for the duration of the day. Activities like reflection can help move mental observations and responses to circumstances. By getting mindful of strain and uneasiness, and interfacing with the breath, the mind will unwind and the body will as well. In any event, removing a couple of seconds from an upsetting day to inhale unobtrusively can have comparative impacts.

Basically, we are what we think, eat, drink, say and relax. Creating and applying care to these parts of life can assist us with maintaining blissful personality body connections. Tell us how you use your mind-body connection with remain sound.

Express your sentiments in proper manners

In the event that sentiments of stress, trouble, or tension are causing physical issues, keeping these emotions inside can aggravate you feel. It's alright to tell your friends and family when something is annoying you. In any case, remember that your loved ones may not generally have the option to assist you with managing your emotions fittingly. On these occasions, approach somebody outside the circumstance for help. Take a stab at asking your family specialist, an instructor, or a strict consultant for guidance and backing to assist you with improving your enthusiastic wellbeing.

Carry on with a healthy lifestyle

Concentrate on the things that you are appreciative of in your life. Do whatever it takes not to fixate on the issues at work, school, or home that lead to negative sentiments. This doesn't mean you need to profess to be cheerful when you feel focused on, on edge, or upset. It's critical to manage these negative emotions, however, attempt to concentrate on the positive things throughout your life, as well. You might need to utilize a diary to monitor things that cause you to feel cheerful or serene. Some exploration has indicated that having an inspirational standpoint can improve your personal satisfaction and give your wellbeing a lift. You may likewise need to discover approaches to relinquish a few things throughout your life that cause you to feel pushed and overpowered. Set aside a few minutes for things you appreciate.

Create strength

Individuals with strength can adapt to worry in a healthy manner. Versatility can be learned and fortified with various methodologies. These incorporate having social help, keeping a positive perspective on yourself, tolerating change, and keeping things in context. An instructor or advisor can assist you with accomplishing this objective with intellectual conduct treatment (CBT). Inquire as to whether this is a smart thought for you.

Quiet your psyche and body

Unwinding techniques, for example, contemplation, tuning in to music, tuning in to guided symbolism tracks, yoga, and Tai Chi are valuable approaches to bring your feelings into balance.

Reflection is a type of guided idea. It can take numerous structures. For instance, you may do it by working out, extending, or breathing profoundly. Approach your family specialist for guidance about unwinding techniques.

Deal with yourself.

To have great passionate wellbeing, it's imperative to deal with your body by having a standard daily schedule for eating well suppers, getting enough rest, and practicing to assuage repressed pressure. Abstain from indulging and don't mishandle medications or liquor, utilizing medications or liquor worthwhile motivations different issues, for example, family and medical issues.

Interesting points

Poor passionate wellbeing can debilitate your body's insusceptible framework. This makes you bound to get colds and different diseases during genuinely troublesome occasions. Additionally, when you are feeling focused on, on edge, or upset, you may not deal with your wellbeing just as you should. You may not want to work out, eating nutritious nourishments, or taking a prescription that your primary care physician endorses. You may mishandle liquor, tobacco, or different medications. Different indications of poor passionate wellbeing include:

- Back torment

- Change in craving

- Chest torment

- Constipation or looseness of the bowels

- Dry mouth

- Extreme tiredness

- General a throbbing painfulness

- Headaches

- High pulse

- Insomnia (inconvenience dozing)

- Lightheadedness

- Palpitations (the inclination that your heart is dashing)

- Sexual issues

- Shortness of breath

- Stiff neck

- Sweating

- Upset stomach

- Weight addition or misfortune

For what reason does my primary care physician need to think about my feelings?

You may not be accustomed to conversing with your primary care physician about your sentiments or issues in your own life. In any case, recollect that the individual in question can't generally tell that you're feeling focused on, on edge, or upset just by taking a gander at you. It's imperative to be straightforward with your primary care physician on the off chance that you are having these sentiments.

In the first place, the person in question should ensure that other medical issues aren't causing your physical side effects. In the event that your side effects aren't brought about by other medical issues, you and your PCP can address the enthusiastic reasons for your manifestations. Your primary care physician may propose approaches to treat your physical manifestations while you cooperate to improve your passionate wellbeing.

Conclusions

The vagus nerve is truly like a magic switch for your body. The fact that it innervates so many major organs and systems emphasizes its importance for your overall health. A vagus nerve that is not toned can cause numerous health problems that are both physical and mental in nature. You might feel pain in various parts of your body as well as depression or irritability. And, all of this can be due to a poorly toned vagus nerve.

The great news is that you can do something about it. You can take active steps to improve your vagus nerve tone in a way that will make your life so much better. You can even assess the tone of your vagus nerve at home, and you can keep track of improvements you make as you go along.

Finally, if you have more serious problems, you can, and should, consult with your doctor. Doctors have numerous ways they can stimulate the vagus nerve, including the implantation of electrical devices. If your health problems are more serious, it will be worth it to speak to your doctor about this type of treatment. And, regardless of the severity of your health problems, it's always advisable to talk to your doctor before implementing any major changes to your activities that might affect your health.

Made in the USA
Coppell, TX
01 June 2022

78360193R00079